HELEN EDMUNDSON

Helen Edmundson was born in Liverpool in 1964 and spent her childhood on the Wirral and in Chester. After studying Drama at Manchester University, she gained wide acting, directing and devising experience with the female agit-prop company, Red Stockings. Her first solo writing attempt, *Ladies in the Lift*, a musical comedy, was created specifically for the company in 1988. On leaving, she worked as an actress in various northwest theatres and on television. Her first play, *Flying*, was presented at the Royal National Theatre Studio in 1990.

Her other work includes: two short television films, *One Day* (BBC, 1991) and *Stella* (Channel 4, 1992); *Anna Karenina* (1992), her first adaptation for Shared Experience Theatre, which won several awards, including the Theatre Managers' Association Award for Best Touring Production; *The Clearing* (1993), first performed at The Bush Theatre, London, joint winner of the John Whiting Award; and *The Mill on the Floss* (1994), her widely acclaimed adaptation for Shared Experience Theatre which won a Time Out Award.

She lives in West London with her husband and son.

A Selection of Other Titles from Nick Hern Books

Anton Chekhov
THE SEAGULL
UNCLE VANYA
(trans Pam Gems)

Caryl Churchill
CHURCHILL: SHORTS
CLOUD NINE
ICECREAM
LIGHT SHINING IN
    BUCKINGHAMSHIRE
MAD FOREST
THE SKRIKER
TRAPS

Jean Cocteau
LES PARENTS TERRIBLES

Ariel Dorfman
DEATH AND THE MAIDEN

Helen Edmundson
ANNA KARENINA
THE CLEARING
THE MILL ON THE FLOSS

Clare McIntyre
MY HEART'S A SUITCASE
    & LOW LEVEL PANIC
THE THICKNESS OF SKIN

Kim Morrissey
DORA

Phyllis Nagy
BUTTERFLY KISS
THE STRIP

Eugene O'Neill
AH! WILDERNESS
ANNA CHRISTIE &
    THE EMPEROR JONES
DESIRE UNDER THE ELMS &
    THE GREAT GOD BROWN
THE HAIRY APE &
    ALL GOD'S CHILLUN
THE ICEMAN COMETH
LONG DAY'S JOURNEY
    INTO NIGHT
A MOON FOR THE
    MISBEGOTTEN
MOURNING BECOMES
    ELECTRA
STRANGE INTERLUDE
A TOUCH OF THE POET

Ludmila Petrushevskaya
CINZANO

Billy Roche
THE CAVALCADERS
THE WEXFORD TRILOGY

Claire Tomalin
THE WINTER WIFE

Sophie Treadwell
MACHINAL

Nicholas Wright
MRS KLEIN

HELEN EDMUNDSON

WAR AND PEACE

Adapted from Tolstoy

NICK HERN BOOKS
London

A Nick Hern Book

This adaptation of *War and Peace* first published
in Great Britain in 1996 as a paperback original by
Nick Hern Books, 14 Larden Road London W3 7ST

War and Peace copyright © 1996 by Helen Edmundson

Helen Edmundson has asserted her moral right to be identified
as author of this work

Front cover photo by Sasha Gusov of Richard Hope and
Anne-Marie Duff in the Royal National Theatre/Shared
Experience production

Typeset by County Setting, Woodchurch, Kent TN26 3TB
Printed by Cox and Wyman Ltd, Reading, Berks

A CIP catalogue record for this book is available from
the British Library

ISBN 1 85459 306 4

Working with Tolstoy

Tolstoy began thinking about the novel which was to become
War and Peace in 1861. His original intention was to write about
a man returning from Siberia, after having been exiled for involve-
ment in the failed Decembrist uprising of 1825. However, as he
constructed the history of this man and the experiences which
brought him to the point of revolution, Tolstoy became increasingly interested in the period 1805-1812, and the book developed
in a different direction. It is consequently not until the first epilogue that we find Pierre (the original 'man') becoming involved
in subversive political activity, and we are left to imagine his fate.

Although coming so late in the novel, this information became key
to my interpretation of it. In the philosophical passages, Tolstoy
sets out clearly, if not dogmatically, a new idea of human freedom:
dismissing free will as an illusion and the exercise of will as futile
and dangerous, he claims that real freedom lies in relinquishing the
will and reconciling ourselves to whatever life brings. This is
borne out in the experiences of his characters, in his depiction of
the struggle between Napoleon and Kutuzov and, finally, verbalised
beautifully and simply by the peasant, Platon Karataev. However,
in leaving us with a Pierre who is rejecting Karataev's wisdom and
preparing to intervene, Tolstoy, almost in spite of himself, admits
that this philosophy is not an easy answer, that it is not an answer
at all for some, and this throws up all sorts of questions which
I felt should be at the centre of the play. Should we make peace
with life and our mortality, or should we fight it to the bitter end?
How can we reconcile ourselves to what is going on around us if
we feel injustice is being done? If we decide to take action, how
can we judge whether it is for the best? Is it ever right for one
person to impose his or her will on others? Even if movements
start in the name of justice and freedom, are they doomed to
become corrupt in the struggle to sustain themselves? These are
dilemmas; ones which are perhaps particularly relevant to our
politically- apathetic and introspective society.

Just a word or two about the specific difficulties of this adaptation.
The number of protagonists in the novel meant that, guided by the
themes of the play, I had to concentrate on some to the detriment
of others. To those whose favourite character seems to have lost

out, I can only apologise. Secondly, I was dealing with the literary depiction of historic fact for the first time, and had to decide how far to adhere to Tolstoy's interpretation of events. I eventually decided that I must do so completely, although I like to think that the introduction of Napoleon's debates with Pierre gives Bonaparte the chance, at least, to put his side of the story. Finally, the fate of Natasha and Maria: every mother knows that the colour of a soiled nappy and the frequency of feeds can become of all-consuming interest when a new baby arrives, but it has always seemed a shame to me that our last glimpse of these spirited women should see them so utterly absorbed in cosy domesticity. There is little I can do about this. In my own epilogue, I have tried to place the emphasis on the danger threatening the happy home, but the fact remains that this is Tolstoy's Natasha and Tolstoy's Maria; he can claim them whenever he wishes, and it is testimony to his genius that they seem so often to exist independently of him. As always when working with Tolstoy, I am left with the impression that he possessed more compassion and humanity than he would ever have cared to admit.

Helen Edmundson
June 1996

War and Peace was co-commissioned by Shared Experience
Theatre and the Royal National Theatre for a co-production in
the Cottesloe. The first preview was given on 8 June 1996 and the
press night was scheduled for 25 June, with the following cast:

Simeon Andrews, Rakie Ayola, Cathryn Bradshaw, Peter de Jersey,
Anne-Marie Duff, David Fielder, Richard Hope, Sam Kelly,
Barbara Marten, Jonathan Oliver, Helen Schlesinger, Joe Stone-
Fewings, Anny Tobin, Ronan Vibert, John Warnaby

THE ATTENDANT	Sam Kelly
PIERRE BEZUHOV	Richard Hope
COUNT ROSTOV	Simeon Andrews
COUNTESS ROSTOV	Barbara Marten
NIKOLAI, their elder son	Joe Stone-Fewings
PETYA, their younger son	Peter de Jersey
NATASHA, their daughter	Anne-Marie Duff
SONYA, a niece of the Rostovs	Cathryn Bradshaw
MARIA DMITRIEVNA, Natasha's godmother	Anny Tobin
PRINCE BOLKONSKY	David Fielder
ANDREI, his son	Ronan Vibert
MARIA, his daughter	Helen Schlesinger
LISA, Prince Andrei's wife	Cathryn Bradshaw
MADEMOISELLE BOURIENNE,	
Princess Maria's French companion	Rakie Ayola
ANNA PAVLOVNA	Anny Tobin
PRINCE VASILI KURAGIN	Jonathan Oliver
ANATOLE, his son	Peter de Jersey
HÉLÈNE, his daughter	Rakie Ayola
GENERAL KUTUZOV,	
Commander in Chief of the Russian Army	Simeon Andrews
NAPOLEON BONAPARTE	John Warnaby
DOLOHOV	Jonathan Oliver
BORIS DRUBETSKOY	John Warnaby
KARATAEV	Sam Kelly

Other parts played by members of the Company.

Music played live by Walter Fabeck (keyboards/music director), Anna Hemery (violin), Roland Melia (cello), Stephen Skinner, (clarinet)

Directors Nancy Meckler and Polly Teale
Designer Bunny Christie
Lighting Chris Davey
Music Peter Salem
Company Movement Liz Ranken
Company Voice Work Patsy Rodenburg

The play was rehearsed with Guy Lankester playing Nikolai. Guy unfortunately broke his ankle during the rehearsal period and had to be replaced. At the time of going to press it is hoped he will rejoin the cast at a future date.

WAR AND PEACE

β

Characters

THE ATTENDANT
PIERRE BEZUHOV
COUNT ROSTOV
COUNTESS ROSTOV
NIKOLAI, *their elder son*
PETYA, *their younger son*
NATASHA, *their daughter*
SONYA, *a niece of the Rostovs*
MARIE DMITRIEVNA, *Natasha's godmother*
PRINCE BOLKONSKY
ANDREI, *his son*
MARIA, *his daughter*
LISA, *Prince Andrei's wife*
MADEMOISELLE BOURIENNE,
     Princess Maria's French companion
ANNA PAVLOVNA
PRINCE VASILI KURAGIN
ANATOLE, *his son*
HELÈNE, *his daughter*
GENERAL KUTUZOV,
     Commander in Chief of the Russian Army
NAPOLEON BONAPARTE
DOLOHOV
BORIS DRUBETSKOV
KARATAEV

Prologue

A gallery in the Hermitage Palace. St. Petersburg. 1996. In one corner, on a wooden chair, an ATTENDANT is sitting, knitting. He has the hunched, worn air of many Russian men.

A younger man (PIERRE) enters. He is wearing bright, fashionable clothes and has a camera round his neck. He looks about the room – up at the fantastic chandeliers and the windows, then at the pictures, in their huge guilt frames. He sees an upholstered, antique chair, and goes to it. He touches the velvety material, then sits.

ATTENDANT (*in Russian*). Don't sit there. It's forbidden. (*In English.*) It's forbidden to sit there.

MAN (*jumping up*). Sorry.

He begins to look at the paintings in more detail.

ATTENDANT (*standing and putting his coat on*). We're closing.

MAN. It's not quite half past.

The ATTENDANT doesn't respond. He puts his knitting away in a carrier bag which displays a picture of a naked woman.

Who are all these men?

ATTENDANT. Officers in the war against Napoleon. 1805 -1812. (*Pointing across the room.*) The Generals are there – Kutuzov, Bagration, Barclay de Tolly. That's Tsar Alexander.

The MAN looks, then goes back to the smaller paintings of the officers.

MAN. These are remarkable. They're all so similar.

ATTENDANT. The same artist. We're closing. (*He goes to the light switch.*)

MAN. And yet each man is there. Each character. Which is your favourite?

ATTENDANT. What's that?

MAN. Which is your favourite one?

The ATTENDANT suddenly blushes, and smiles like a child. He comes over to the man, bashfully.

ATTENDANT. I love them all. I have been sitting here every day for many years. They are my friends.

MAN. Why are some of them missing? Restoration?

ATTENDANT. No. They were the officers who took part in the failed revolution. The Decembrists.

MAN. I don't know anything about that.

ATTENDANT. 1825. An uprising of officers and intellectuals against the new Tsar Nicholas. The leaders were hanged. Others were banished to Siberia. Portraits of offenders were removed.

MAN. You have to admire them. To raise your hand against all this . . .

ATTENDANT. We fight and fight for what we believe in. And because we believe in it we think it is right.

Music. Gradually through the scene, the characters of the play begin to filter into the room and inhabit it.

Your first time in St. Petersburg?

MAN. Yes. My ancestors were Russian.

ATTENDANT. No-one ever stops in here. Right now they all rush through, looking for the paintings recovered from the Nazis. Next year it will be something else. Yes, everything is always shifting, shifting. The lady of the court who once sat in that chair, would never have believed that her God, the Tsar would one day be torn from this palace and killed. The men in those missing paintings would never have believed that one day Stalin's image would be wiped like a stain from the face of Russia. Go to the Literary Museum. Take a taxi, the bus is too democratic. Look at the statue of Gorki. Three months ago, that was a statue of Lenin – but they trimmed the moustache a little, added a lot of hair . . . (*The* MAN *laughs.*) We are all bound by time. Only the Lord is free.

MAN. You weren't always an attendant, were you?

ATTENDANT. You are right, my friend.

MAN. Are you happy?

ATTENDANT. Yes, why not? It is warm in here, the canteen is good. My wife sells our knitting in the Metro at weekends. Why not happy? When I lie on my death bed, will I think of Stalin, or Yeltsin or Gorbachov? No. It is love which endures. Perhaps I will think of you though, because we talked unexpectedly today. I will think of you because you asked me which painting I like best.

The music rises. The characters, past and present, begin to move slowly forward, as if into battle. Suddenly one of them cries out – 'charge' – and all rush forward with a mixture of aggression and fear. They disband.

Act One

Scene 1

ANNA PAVLOVNA SCHERER's *house, St. Petersburg.*

The guests at her soirée divide into several liquid groups, with
LISA *seated at the centre of one and* HELÈNE *at the centre of*
another towards the back of the stage.

PIERRE *stands in the middle, looking about in anticipation like a*
child in a toy shop. PRINCE VASILI *has a strong grasp on his*
arm. ANNA PAVLOVNA SCHERER *approaches.*

VASILI. Anna Pavlovna, ma chère hostesse, if you can knock this
    bear into shape for me, I will be your most devoted slave. He
    has been staying with me for a month now and has spent every
    moment with my recalcitrant son. This is the first time he's set
    forth into society.

ANNA. Then, Prince Vasili, we must see what we can do.

VASILI. Nothing is so necessary for a young man as the company
    of clever women, and you are the cleverest woman in St.
    Petersburg.

ANNA. Flatterer.

He kisses her hand and leaves to join another group. PIERRE
tries to follow him, but ANNA PAVLOVNA *restrains him.*

It is very good of you, Monsieur Pierre, to come and visit a
poor invalid. (*She pauses, expecting a reply but* PIERRE *is not*
listening.) Not that I am suffering greatly, it is merely an attack
of 'la grippe', similar to that endured by the Dowager Empress.

PIERRE. What's that? I'm so sorry . . .

ANNA (*drawing him towards a rather dull-looking group in a*
    corner). Please come and meet my aunt.

LISA (*calling across the room*). Annette, Annette, do come. The
    Vicomte is going to tell us about the duc d'Enghien.

ANNA. Ah yes. Contez-nous çela, Vicomte. Do come and listen
    everyone.

A small crowd gathers. PIERRE *is forced to the back.*

ANNA (*confidentially to guests*). The Vicomte knew the duc
    personally.

LISA. Wait a moment till I get my work out. (*To the man beside her.*) Pass me my reticule.

ANNA. The Vicomte is the best kind of emigré, a most profound thinker. Hélène, chère Hélène, do join us.

HÉLÈNE *turns, smiles and rises. Everyone falls silent as she floats forward majestically and takes the seat vacated for her opposite the* VICOMTE. PIERRE *is transfixed. Someone whispers, 'What a charming creature'.*

VICOMTE. Madame, I doubt my ability in the face of such an audience.

HÉLÈNE *merely smiles and waits.*

OLD AUNT. I hope it isn't a ghost story.

LISA. There now. I am quite ready. You may begin.

VICOMTE. I have it on the most reliable information that the duc d'Enghien returned secretly to Paris, not to effect political discontent, but simply to enjoy the favours of the celebrated actress, Mademoiselle Georges. Whilst waiting in an ante-chamber, he heard a door open and before he had chance to conceal himself, saw a small figure emerging from her room. In a moment, he realised to his horror that it was none other than his enemy Napoleon Bonaparte, who, recognizing in turn the duc, fell into one of the swoons to which he is subject. The duc, being evidently a gentleman, took no advantage of his position and, laying Napoleon on a chair, left the house. In doing this he made a fatal mistake: Bonaparte could not forgive the fact that the duc had witnessed his mortality. He had him tracked down, kidnapped and executed in the space of a week.

LISA. Charming.

GUEST. Charming. Beautifully told.

ANNA. Really. It is too much. Surely the world cannot stand by any longer and condone the atrocities perpetrated by that Antichrist. Anyone who refuses to accept that we must go to war is no longer a friend of mine.

VASILI. Dear Annette, such eloquence. You frighten us.

ANNA. The one thing I have faith in is that our fine and virtuous Emperor Alexander will step in where all the other sovereigns of Europe have failed. He will crush the hydra of revolution and rid the world of this Corsican monster.

PIERRE. The execution of the duc d'Enghien was a political necessity.

There is a stunned silence. Someone giggles.

ATTENDANT (*announcing*). Prince Andrei Bolkonsky.

PRINCE ANDREI *enters*. ANNA PAVLOVNA *seizes upon him*.

ANNA. Ah, Prince André, you are here at last. You know almost everyone, I'm sure. Lise has been telling us how you think of enlisting for the war.

LISA. He doesn't care about me, do you André? He is leaving me quite alone in the country.

ANDREI *does not answer*. HÉLÈNE *stands. All the men follow*.

HÉLÈNE. Papa, we shall be late.

VASILI. Ah yes. You will excuse us, my dear Vicomte, this wretched reception at the Ambassador's, you know.

HÉLÈNE *moves towards the door. Everyone makes way for her*.

ANNA. She is really very beautiful, Vasili. Even at Court they say she is as lovely as the day. It hardly seems fair that you should have two such splendid children.

VASILI. To be honest with you, they are the bane of my existence. My son cost me forty thousand roubles last year. He will ruin me.

ANNA. You must make sure they marry and marry well. They do say old maids have a mania for matchmaking. I shall begin with your family.

PRINCE VASILI *kisses her hand and leaves with his daughter*.

PIERRE *approaches* ANDREI *who is watching* HÉLÈNE.

PIERRE. Very pretty, eh?

ANDREI *looks round, annoyed, but seeing* PIERRE *he smiles*.

ANDREI. Very.

PIERRE. Not for the likes of me, though.

ANDREI. What on earth are you doing here?

PIERRE. I knew I'd find you. I thought I could come to supper with you. May I?

ANDREI. Absolutely not.

He smiles, and PIERRE *understands that he is joking. They join the group around the* VICOMTE.

VICOMTE. If Bonaparte remains on the throne another year, things will have gone too far. By intrigue and executions, French society will have been destroyed forever.

ANNA. Have no fear, my dear Vicomte. The Emperor Alexander in his benevolence will leave it to the French people to choose their own form of government, and it is certain that the whole nation, once delivered from the usurper, will throw itself into the arms of its rightful king.

ANDREI. I'm afraid I agree with Monsieur le Vicomte. It would be difficult to return to the old regime.

PIERRE. From what I heard in Paris, almost all the aristocracy has gone over to Bonaparte.

There is a frisson in the room. All look at the VICOMTE.

VICOMTE. That is what the Bonapartists say. Although, since the murder of the duc, I cannot believe even Bonaparte's most ardent supporters regard him as a hero.

PIERRE. The execution of the duc was a political necessity and I consider that Napoleon showed nobility of soul in not hesitating to assume responsibility.

ANNA. Dieu! Mon Dieu!

LISA. What, Monsieur Pierre, do you think murder a proof of nobility of soul?

OLD AUNT. Capital!

PIERRE. I say so because the Bourbons fled the revolution, leaving the people to anarchy. Napoleon alone was capable of quelling it and for the general good he could not stop short at the life of one man.

ANNA. Won't you come over to the other table?

PIERRE. Yes! Napoleon is great because he towered above the revolution, suppressed its abuses, preserved all that was good in it – equality of citizenship, freedom of speech and of the press . . .

ANNA. Whatever next? Won't you come over to this . . .

PIERRE. The whole meaning of the revolution lay in the rights of man, in emancipation from prejudice, in liberty and equality.

VICOMTE. High sounding words that have long been debased. Who does not love liberty and equality? The people wanted liberty but Bonaparte destroyed it!

PIERRE. The revolution was a grand fact!

Scene 2

PRINCE BOLKONSKY's *estate* (*Bald Hills.*) *50 miles from Moscow.*

MARIA *stands in the doorway of the ante-chamber to her father's study. She has an exercise book in her hand. Her features are strained and her breathing uneven. She crosses herself.*

MARIA (*whispering*). Oh Lord, grant me courage and humility now and forever more.

PRINCE BOLKONSKY is sitting at his lathe, turning the treadle with his embroidered silver boot. The rhythmic hum of the machine breaks the studied silence of the old house.

The ATTENDANT *is sitting in the ante-chamber. He stands.*

ATTENDANT. Good evening, Princess Maria.

MARIA. Good evening.

He stands aside as she timidly enters her father's presence.

The PRINCE *glances at her but goes on with his work for several seconds before stopping and moving to a table where some large books are lying open and a chair awaits.*

PRINCE B. Two minutes late.

MARIA. Sorry Father.

PRINCE B. Come here then. (*She does so.*) Sit down.

He takes the exercise book and checks her work.

Here you have written eight where you should have written eighty.

MARIA (*rigid with nerves*). Oh yes. Sorry.

PRINCE B (*seeming satisfied.*) Well then, today's lesson. (*He leans over her to look at a book.*) Now madam, you will observe that the two triangles are of different types. Given that the sum of the angles of each must equal what . . . ?

MARIA. *is breathing so heavily and her heart is beating so loudly that she can hardly hear him.*

Must equal what? (*Pause.*) Must equal what? (*He struggles physically to control his agitation.*) Well, madam? The sum of the angles must equal what?

MARIA (*stumbling over the word*). Isosceles?

PRINCE B. Good God, the girl is an idiot!

He slams the book down on the table and paces the room. Once calmer, he returns and touches MARIA's *hair gently. Her crisis subsides somewhat.*

Well then, well then. This won't do. Take it. Prepare it for tomorrow. Mathematics is a most important subject, madam. It will drive all the nonsense from your head. I won't have you being a fool like the rest of your sex. Do you wish to be a fool?

MARIA. No, Father.

PRINCE B. Well then.

MARIA *waits for a moment and then turns to go*.

Wait. This came for you. (*He holds out a book.*) From one of your religious crowd in Moscow. I haven't read it. Letters I shall always read but a book like this is your own concern.

MARIA. You may read it if you wish, Father.

PRINCE B. I said I will not read it. I don't interfere with a person's beliefs. Or are you trying to bring me to the fold again?

MARIA. No, Father.

PRINCE B. Good. Because you're wasting your time. Now be off with you. (*He walks her to the door and pats her shoulder.*) Be off.

MARIA *leaves him. She stands in the ante-chamber and breathes a deep breath.*

MARIA (*whispering to* ATTENDANT). Thank you. If anyone needs me I will be in the chapel.

MLLE BOURIENNE *approaches*.

MLLE B (*loudly*). Ah, Princess Maria. (*She realises she must lower her voice and does so.*) I was just coming to warn you. Apparently the Prince has been shouting horribly at the bailiff all afternoon. He is in a very bad humour, très mauvais . . .

MARIA. My dear Mademoiselle, I have asked you never to call attention to the humour in which my father happens to be. I do not allow myself to criticize him, and would not have others do so.

She walks off quickly, leaving MLLE BOURIENNE *standing*.

Scene 3

The ROSTOV *house, Moscow*.

At first we are only aware of NATASHA, *who is standing in the middle of the drawing room, singing. She is concentrating and seems serious and intense. A few moments later however, she begins to laugh and cannot go on with the song. There is laughter all around her and we become aware of her family –* COUNT *and* COUNTESS ROSTOV, NIKOLAI, PETYA *and* SONYA, *along with* BORIS *and* MARIA DMITRIEVNA.

NATASHA. Petya! Petya was making me laugh.

COUNTESS. Do stop it, Petya. Stop it, all of you.

COUNT. Go on, go on my little pet, it sounded splendid.

COUNTESS. Don't spoil her, Ilya.

COUNT. What a voice, eh, Maria Dmitrievna? Her Italian teacher thinks we have a second Salomoni in our midst. What do you think, eh?

MARIA D. What do I think, you old sinner? I think if she puts on such a performance at her name-day party, she'll disgrace us all and I shall be ashamed to call myself her Godmother.

COUNTESS. Quite right.

NATASHA. Oh, I won't laugh then. I won't.

MARIA D. The eyes of all Moscow will be on you, Natasha Rostova, trying to decide if you are a young woman or a child still . . .

NIKOLAI. A child, definitely a child.

MARIA D. And it won't take anyone long to decide 'child' and a Cossack to boot.

NATASHA. I'll do it now. I'll do it properly.

All go quiet. She manages a few notes then laughs again.

COUNTESS. Natasha! Really.

NIKOLAI. We can sing a duet if you like, little sister.

NATASHA. No, no, I'm doing it on my own. (*She suddenly holds up her doll.*) I know: Mimi can do it.

COUNT. Splendid idea!

BORIS. No she can't, Natasha. Not since her accident.

COUNTESS. What accident?

BORIS. Didn't you hear, Countess Rostova? A tragedy. Cracked her head open on a plant pot in the conservatory.

NATASHA. Boris!

BORIS. Very nasty business. Quite ruined her looks.

COUNTESS. I think we had better leave the singing for today.

NATASHA. Are you coming to my party, Maria Dmitrievna?

MARIA D. Of course. Someone has to keep you in hand.

NATASHA. Are you going to dance?

MARIA D. Indeed I am not.

COUNT. Oh come now, come now, I daresay after one or two glasses of my best Madeira, someone will tempt you to the floor.

MARIA D. They will not, you know.

NATASHA. I'm going to be a dancer.

PETYA. You said you were going to be a singer.

COUNTESS. It's time you were in bed, Petya.

MARIA D. And Nikolai is going to be a soldier, I hear.

COUNT. Ah yes. Boris here has been given his commission, so for friendship's sake Nikolai throws up the university and deserts his old father to go into the army. The Hussars!

NIKOLAI. It's not out of friendship at all. The army is my vocation.

COUNT. Yes, yes.

NIKOLAI. I've already told you Papa, if you really don't want me to go I'll stay. But I'd be no use anywhere except the army. I'm just not a diplomat or a government clerk, I'm no good at disguising my feelings.

MARIA D. Good for you, boy.

COUNT. Ah well. I doubt he'll see action anyway.

BORIS. In St. Petersburg they say war has been declared.

COUNT. They've been saying so for a long while and they will say so again and again and then that will be the end of it.

COUNTESS. He will look very smart in his uniform. All the young heiresses will be falling at his feet.

SONYA *who, up until now has been basking in* NIKOLAI's *glory suddenly turns pale.* NIKOLAI *glances at her uneasily.*

NIKOLAI. Mother, please . . . . That's hardly the point.

COUNTESS. We shall have you married in no time.

MARIA. D. If you want my opinion we will be at war, and sooner rather than later. But that's all the more reason to go. I have four sons in the army but still I don't fret. You may die in your bed or God may bring you safely out of battle. It's all in his hands.

SONYA *suddenly runs from the room.*

NATASHA. Now look what you've done.

COUNTESS. Natasha!

NATASHA (*running after her*). Sonya, wait.

MARIA D. Cossack!

Scene 4

The study. ANDREI's *house. St. Petersburg.*

NAPOLEON *is standing in the shadows.* PIERRE *is pacing the room, imitating* NAPOLEON *making a speech.*

PIERRE. England's day is over!

PIERRE makes a large gesture. NAPOLEON demonstrates how it should be done.

England's day is over! (*He gestures. NAPOLEON nods approval.*) They said la Manche could not be crossed – I have crossed it! (*Again NAPOLEON corrects his gesture.*) They said that London would never fall – she has fallen to me! Mr Pitt, as a traitor to your country and the rights of man, I sentence you . . .

ANDREI enters. NAPOLEON disappears. PIERRE sits – quickly.

ANDREI. What have you done to poor Anna Pavlovna? You're going to have to learn, my dear friend, that there's a time and a place for speaking one's mind.

PIERRE. Oh dear. Was I that bad?

They both smile. ANDREI settles in his chair.

ANDREI. So tell me, what career have you decided on?

PIERRE. I haven't.

ANDREI. Your father's waiting for an answer, isn't he? How is he?

PIERRE. Still very ill, I believe. You know, that Vicomte was interesting but . . .

ANDREI. Don't change the subject. Have you thought about the Horseguards?

PIERRE. No. Actually, I've got a problem with this war. If it were a war for freedom, I'd have been the first to join the army, but to help England and Austria against the greatest man on earth – it's not right.

ANDREI. If we all felt we had to believe in the cause we were fighting for, there would be no wars.

PIERRE. And a very good thing too.

ANDREI. Probably. But it will never happen.

PIERRE. So tell me, I don't understand: what are you going to war for?

ANDREI. What for?

PIERRE. Yes.

ANDREI. Because I have to. And I'm going . . . well, let's just say I'm going because my life here is not to my taste.

LISA enters.

LISA. Dear oh dear, Monsieur Pierre, what a contentious person you are.

PIERRE. I'm afraid I was just arguing again. I can't work out why your husband wants to go to the war.

LISA. But that's exactly what I say! I just can't understand why men can't survive without war. If it were left to women there would be nothing of the kind. Do tell him, mon cher. You know, if he would only stay here, he is on the edge of a brilliant career. Only today I heard a lady ask, 'Is that the famous Prince André?' I did really.

PIERRE *notices the rigid expression on* ANDREI's *face*.

PIERRE (*gently*). When do you leave?

LISA. Oh please don't talk about that, I can't bear it. On a whim, a mere whim, he is deserting me and shutting me up alone in the country.

ANDREI. You will not be alone. You will be with my father and sister. Maria will take care of you.

LISA. But I will not see any of my friends. And then, you know André, I am frightened.

ANDREI (*struggling to be polite*). What are you frightened of, Lise? I don't understand.

LISA. No. I don't suppose you do. I have to say . . . you have changed. You have changed terribly.

ANDREI. Your doctor said you should go to bed earlier.

LISA *doesn't move. She is on the verge of tears.*

LISA. Why should I care if Monsieur Pierre is here? I have been wanting to ask you for a long time why you have changed towards me. What have I done? You are going off to war without a thought of what it might mean to me. Why? Why, André?

ANREI. Lise.

LISA. You treat me like an invalid or a child. You certainly weren't like this six months ago.

PIERRE. Please don't upset yourself, Princess. (*He stands.*) Excuse me, an outsider has no business here.

ANREI No wait, Pierre. The Princess is so kind, she would not wish to deprive me of your company.

LISA. Oh, of course, we are thinking only of you again, never of me.

ANDREI. Lise!

LISA (*shocked into submission by his severity*). Mon Dieu! Mon Dieu!

ANDREI. Bonsoir, Lise.

He rises and kisses her hand as if she were a stranger. She leaves. There is a long silence.

Never, never marry, my dear fellow. Don't marry until you've stopped loving the woman of your choice and seen her as she really is. You are surprised. My wife is an excellent woman, one of those rare women with a whom a man's honour is safe, but, my God, what wouldn't I give not to be married. My father is right: selfish, vain, banal, that's what women are. When you see them in society, you might fancy they had something in them but there is nothing, nothing. I would never say this to anyone else, you understand? You talk of Bonaparte, but Bonaparte was free when he worked his way towards his goal. There was nothing for him but his goal and he reached it. But tie yourself to a woman and, like a convict in irons, you lose all freedom. And all your aspirations, all the ability you feel within yourself, become nothing but a source of regret, a torture. Drawing rooms, gossip, balls, that is the enchanted circle I move in now. I am setting off to take part in the greatest war there ever was and I know nothing and am fit for nothing. I am an amiable fellow with a caustic wit.

PIERRE. Andrei . . . that you of all people should consider yourself a failure . . . I admire you more than anyone I know. I mean, you are everything I am not. You have strength of mind, you have will power. You could achieve anything you desire.

ANDREI. My day is done. What is there to say about me? We were talking about you.

PIERRE. What is there to say about me? What am I? The bastard son of a wealthy man. Oh, I'm grateful to my father; at least he's given me an education. But I'm not a boy anymore and I'm back and . . . what? I can't use his name without blushing, I have no fortune. In Paris I was inspired. I dreamt of setting up a republic in Russia, I dreamt of spreading all that's great in Napoleon's ideas.

ANDREI. So why don't you?

PIERRE. You know me. Now that I'm back it's all I can do to get out of bed before one o'clock. I seem to be drunk all the time, and then there's the women . . . I don't know what to do, Andrei.

ANDREI. Listen to me: you're lucky. You are the one live soul in all our circle of acquaintance. You'll be all right no matter what because you are alive. Don't waste it.

Pause.

PIERRE. You're right. Of course, you're right. I was supposed to go out tonight but I won't. I won't go.

ANDREI. Give me your word of honour.

PIERRE. My word of honour.

Scene 5

The chapel. Bald Hills. MARIA is kneeling in prayer.

MARIA. I walked through the estate this morning. I saw a convoy of conscripts on their way to the army. The men's faces were blank but the mothers and wives and children were sobbing and clinging to them and falling to their knees in the dust on the road. Please keep them in your care. It seems the war is even to touch us here. It seems as though humanity has forgotten the precepts of its divine Saviour who preached love and forgiveness of injuries.

Oh Lord, thank you for my peace. Thank you for my quiet corner. I sometimes feel I live in a convent with all the privilege and none of the hardship. Thank you for my father's love which surrounds me always. I do love him. I could not be happier.

The figure of a MAN has appeared in the room. His features are indistinct. MARIA knows he is there but does not look at him, even though he has come very close.

What more can I ask from life than to spend each day as I do now, in contemplation of the sublime principles which our divine Saviour, left for our guidance here below?

He touches her.

Help me to adhere to those principles and never let my mind seek to . . .

She gives in and turns. They embrace and are momentarily lost in passion. This is MARIA's fantasy – one in which she is carried away into a new life and earthly love by a handsome stranger.

She suddenly breaks away from him.

No. No.

He disappears. She falls to her knees.

Oh God, help me to stifle in my heart these temptings of the Devil, so as to fulfil Thy will on earth. Oh Lord, forgive me. Thank you for my peace.

Scene 6

The ROSTOV *house. Moscow.*

NATASHA *enters a room which would appear to be empty but for the sound of sobbing. The source of the noise is* SONYA, *who is sitting in a corner.* NATASHA *runs to her and begins to cry too.*

NATASHA. Oh Sonya, Sonya, please don't cry. Is it because Nikolai is going away?

SONYA. I do love Nikolai, Natasha . . .

NATASHA. I know you do.

SONYA. But your mother will never let us marry, because we are cousins.

NATASHA. Oh Sonya . . .

SONYA. The Archbishop himself would have to say we could and it's all impossible and I haven't any fortune and your mother wants him to marry an . . . heiress.

NATASHA. But Nikolai loves you. He won't marry an heiress.

SONYA (*showing the piece of paper in her hand*). He wrote these verses for me. They're so beautiful, but if your mother saw them she would be angry. But I love her so much too. She's the only mother I've ever known and she took me in when no-one else wanted me.

NATASHA. Oh my pet, my darling, don't cry. Don't you remember what we were saying, after supper the other evening? We decided how it will all be. You will marry Nikolai and I will marry Boris and we will all live in the same house.

SONYA. But mother . . .

NATASHA. Nikolai will tell Mama that he is going to marry you and that's all.

SONYA. Do you think so? Really and truly?

NATASHA. Really and truly.

SONYA. Oh Natasha.

They embrace and laugh. There is the sound of footsteps.

NATASHA. He's coming.

NATASHA *darts away and hides as* NIKOLAI *enters.*

SONYA. Natasha, don't go . . .

NIKOLAI. What's the matter? Why did you run away?

SONYA. Oh, it's nothing. I was just being silly.

NIKOLAI (*taking her hand*). Was it because of what Mama said? Sonya, how can you listen to her? You know you mean more to me than the whole world.

SONYA. I don't want you to say things like that.

NIKOLAI. Well, I won't then. But I'll prove it.

He draws her to him and kisses her on the lips. Then he leads her away. NATASHA *emerges from her hiding place.*

NATASHA. Ooo, how delicious!

BORIS *enters – right on cue.*

Boris, come here, I want to tell you something.

BORIS. What is it?

NATASHA. Come here.

He approaches. She holds up Mimi.

Kiss Mimi. (BORIS *gives a puzzled laugh.*) Don't you want to? Well come here then. (*She draws him into the corner.*) Closer. Closer. Would you like to kiss me?

BORIS (*blushing*). Natasha . . . really!

NATASHA *jumps onto the chest, and, flinging her arms around his neck, kisses him smack on the lips. She gets down and stands with her head lowered.*

BORIS. Oh . . . Oh. Natasha, please, you know that I love you but . . .

NATASHA. Are you in love with me?

BORIS. Yes I am. But please, let's not do this again. We must wait. We must wait for another four years and then I will ask for your hand.

NATASHA (*counting on her fingers*). Thirteen, fourteen, fifteen. sixteen. All right then. That's settled.

BORIS. Yes. Settled.

NATASHA. For ever and ever until we die.

Scene 7

ANATOLE's *rooms. St. Petersburg.*

PIERRE. *enters to find a room full of men. They are shouting, laughing, drinking, arguing. Here and there, women are visible and, at the centre of one group, a bear-cub tethered to a chain is being teased and goaded. One man – DOLOHOV – is standing on the sill of a large window, from which the frame has been wrenched out, looking down defiantly at the crowd. Men shout up to him – 'No holding on' – 'I back him' etc.*

A tall handsome man sees PIERRE *and embraces him clumsily.*

ANATOLE. Pierre.

PIERRE. Anatole.

ANATOLE. You're late. (*He gives him a glass of wine.*)

PIERRE. I promised someone I wouldn't come but then I'd
already promised you that I would so . . . never mind. What's
going on? Dolohov, what are you doing?

ANATOLE. Wait, you're not drunk yet.

ANATOLE *makes* PIERRE *drink several glasses in succession.*

DOLOHOV (*announcing*). I wager fifty imperials – fifty – that I
will sit outside this window, here, without holding on to
anything and drink this whole bottle of rum without taking it
from my lips. If anyone else will do it after me, I'll pay him one
hundred imperials.

There is a roar of approbation. A YOUNG MAN *goes to the
window and looks down.*

MAN. Oh-h-h, not likely.

DOLOHOV. Shut-up.

*He pushes him away, violently. Then he climbs through the
casement carefully and settles himself in a sitting position. He
takes his hands away.*

OLD MAN (*rushing towards him*). Gentlemen this is madness,
he'll be killed.

ANATOLE (*restraining him*). Don't touch him.

DOLOHOV. If anyone does that again, I'll send him to his death.

DOLOHOV *steadies himself and raises the bottle to his lips.*
PIERRE *covers his eyes as everything goes into slow-motion.*

The crowd clap. The older man cannot look. PIERRE *uncovers
his eyes for a moment and* DOLOHOV *almost slips.* PIERRE
gasps. Suddenly it is all over. DOLOHOV *stands and turns to
face the room.*

DOLOHOV. Empty!

There is a cry of 'bravo'. DOLOHOV *jumps down and stands
frowning and silent.* PIERRE *dashes to the window.*

PIERRE. Who wants to bet with me? I'm doing it now. I'll do it
without a bet.

ANATOLE. Don't be ridiculous. You get giddy just walking
downstairs.

DOLOHOV. Let him do it if he wants to.

But several men try to stop PIERRE *climbing onto the sill.*

PIERRE. Give me a bottle. Get off me . . .

He is so strong that he sends them all flying.

ANATOLE. You'll never stop him like that. Wait. (*He grabs a woman.*) Pierre? Pierre?

PIERRE. What?

ANATOLE. I'll take your bet but for tomorrow. Right now we've got something better to do.

PIERRE. Yes! Wait! I'm coming. (*He jumps down.*) Wait.

Act Two

Scene 1

The ballroom. The ROSTOV *house, Moscow.*

There are mirrors around the room, shining in the light of the chandeliers. NATASHA *enters and dances, admiring herself in the glass. She sings in an operatic voice.*

NATASHA. Isn't that Natasha Rostova? Yes, and isn't she exquisite? They say that every young man in Russia is in love with her, but she is secretly engaged to Boris Drubetskoy. (*She feigns a gasp of shock.*).

COUNT *and* COUNTESS ROSTOV *enter, pursued by* NIKOLAI. SONYA *follows.* NIKOLAI *is in uniform. He is reading aloud from the Tsar's manifesto on the declaration of war. The* COUNTESS *is silent and keeps her back to him.*

NIKOLAI. 'The Emperor can no longer view with indifference the danger threatening our beloved country. The safety and dignity of the Empire, the sanctity of our alliances and the desire which constitutes the Emperor's sole aim – to establish peace in Europe – have now decided him to move part of his army across the frontier into Austria.'

Pause.

COUNT (*suddenly*). Why the deuce should we have to fight Bonaparte? It will end in tears, you know. Look at what he has done to Austria. And Suvorov! The greatest general in our history was hacked to pieces, and where shall we find another Suvorov these days?

NATASHA. Are we going to war?

NIKOLAI. I can't believe you mean that, Father. The answer is here. (*He brandishes the manifesto.*) We Russians must fight to the last drop of our blood. I, for one, am willing to die for my Emperor.

The COUNT *irately and silently indicates to* NIKOLAI *to be quiet on account of his mother.* SONYA *takes* NIKOLAI's *hand and looks at him in admiration.*

Colonel Schubert is coming to Natasha's party tonight. I will leave with him. (*He wants to say something to his mother but thinks better of it.*). Well then. I shall go and prepare.

NIKOLAI and SONYA leave.

COUNT. He's right, of course. He's a young man. It would make him ashamed to stay and we don't want that, do we? (*He puts an arm tentatively around his wife.*) Don't be sad, my little Countess. He'll be back before we know it. Must get on. What a sauté of game au madère we are going to have, Natasha! That new chef is well worth the money.

He leaves.

NATASHA. Mother? You're not crying are you?

COUNTESS. When I was carrying him, when he was lying somewhere under my heart, I couldn't believe . . . I just couldn't believe that one day he would . . . live, that he would cry and cling to my breast and that one day he would talk. Talk! And now he's a man. And I can't believe that either. He will play men's games and live in a man's world where . . . where I can't be. That's all. That's all.

Scene 2

The drawing room. Bald Hills.

MARIA *is practising the clavier.* LISA *enters on tip-toe.* MLLE BOURIENNE *hovers behind her.* LISA *giggles.* MARIA *looks round and gives a cry of delight. The two women fall into each other's arms, kissing each other's hands and faces, laughing and crying.* MLLE BOURIENNE *looks on, smiling tearfully.* ANDREI *enters and stands in the doorway.*

LISA. Weren't you expecting us?

MARIA. Oh yes, but . . .

LISA. This place is a palace, Marie. I had no idea.

MARIA (*looking with delight at* LISA's *round figure*). How long is there to go?

LISA. A few months yet.

MARIA (*noticing* ANDREI). Andrei! I didn't see you.

She runs to him and he kisses her fondly.

ANDREI. Still the cry-baby, I see.

LISA. Take no notice of him. He can't abide tears, you know. He is quite changed of late.

MARIA. Are you really going to the war, Andrei?

ANDREI. General Kutuzov has made me his aide-de-camp. I must leave tonight.

LISA. He is abandoning me here for no reason at all. If he would only stay in St. Petersburg he would win promotion . . .

ANDREI. Lise needs to rest. Perhaps you could show my wife to her room, Maria, while I go and see Father. How is he?

MARIA. Just the same. You might notice some change.

ANDREI. I'll see you at dinner.

He leaves. LISA *begins to cry.*

MARIA. Lise, what is it?

MLLE BOURIENNE. She is tired after the journey, perhaps.

LISA. He is so cold. And so cruel.

MARIA *directs* MLLE BOURIENNE *to leave them. She does so.*

He has changed so much. He hates me. Everything I do makes him angry.

MARIA. I'm sure that isn't true.

LISA. And he doesn't understand at all how frightened I am about . . . about . . .

MARIA. About the baby?

LISA *nods and sobs uncontrollably.*

Don't, don't, my darling. I know Andrei cares for you very much. If he seems cold sometimes . . .

LISA. All the time.

MARIA. Well . . . perhaps he is frightened too.

LISA. What has he to be frightened of? Oh, Marie! I have been so unhappy.

MARIA. Dear Lise, you mustn't be afraid. We have been looking forward to your visit so much. And my father is so kind. Don't cry, now. Don't cry.

Scene 3

The dining room. Bald Hills.

MARIA, ANDREI, LISA *and* MLLE BOURIENNE *are awaiting the* PRINCE. *The* ATTENDANT *is poised, ready to serve dinner. The clock strikes eight. The old* PRINCE *enters. His eyes settle on* LISA, *who almost trembles under his scrutiny. He approaches her and pats her awkwardly on the back of the neck.*

PRINCE B. I am glad, glad to see you. Sit down! Sit down, everyone. Mlle Bourienne, sit down!

MLLE BOURIENNE. Thank you, your Excellency.

All take their seats quickly.

PRINCE B *(looking at* LISA's *tummy).* Oh ho! Someone's been in a hurry, I see. Too bad! You must take plenty of exercise. None of this lounging on sofas. Walk! Walk as much as possible.

There is an uneasy silence. LISA *is confused.* MARIA *is nervous for her.* ANDREI *enjoys his father's performance.*

And how are the shining lights of Petersburg society?

LISA *(relieved).* Oh, Anna Pavlovna Scherer had an attack of la grippe last week, but she is quite recovered now.

PRINCE B. God be praised!

LISA. Indeed. I never miss her soirées. You know, I was saying to André only the other day, I can't think how it is that Annette never married. You men really have no sense where women are concerned. Prince Vasili Kuragin sends you his respects.

PRINCE B. His respects to me? I am honoured.

LISA. Oh yes. He expressly said so. Countess Apraksin, poor thing, has lost her husband. She cried her eyes out.

PRINCE B. Most unfortunate, to lose one's husband, so shortly followed by one's eyes.

LISA. And you would not believe who Kitty Odyntsov has married: old Prince Ryevsky! Why he is so, well . . .

PRINCE B. Old?

LISA. Yes! Everyone was quite shocked. I hope we shan't be in society here, because André made me leave all my good dresses in Petersburg. This tired article is the best I can do.

The PRINCE *suddenly turns away from her.*

PRINCE B. Well, Mademoiselle, it looks as though your friend Napoleon is in for a bad time: Prince Andrei here, is setting out to conquer him. *(Singing.)* 'Malbrook s'en va-t-en guerre, Dieu sait quand reviendra.' Games! That's all it is. There are no political complications in Europe. It is a sordid little puppet-show played out by fools with nothing better to do. Our generals are schoolboys. Kutuzov knows something, he fought beside me under Suvorov, but as for the rest of them! And Bonaparte is a trumped-up little Frenchy who has only won so far because he's stuck to fighting Germans. From the very beginning of the world everyone has beaten the Germans! Apologies my dear Mlle. *(Confidentially to others.)* She is a great admirer of Bonaparte.

MLLE BOURIENNE. You know I am no Bonapartist, sir.

ANDREI. Father, you may be right about our leaders and I daresay our plans aren't perfect but, scoff as you will, Bonaparte is a great general.

PRINCE B. What has he done that is so great?

ANDREI. He beat your great Suvorov, for one.

PRINCE B. Suvorov! (*He flings his plate away. The* ATTENDANT *catches it.*) Suvorov! Suvorov was saddled with the Austrians. The Devil himself could do nothing saddled with the Hofs-kriegs-wurst-schnapps-raths!

ANDREI. We shall be saddled with the Austrians.

PRINCE B. Then that is why you will lose. Not because of any genius on the part of your powder-monkey emperor. My apologies, Mademoiselle. (*Singing.*) 'Malbrook s'en va-t-en guerre, Dieu sait quand reviendra.' Eh, Maria?

Scene 4

The ballroom. The ROSTOV *house. Moscow.*

It is NATASHA's *party and the room is full of people.* NATASHA, NIKOLAI *and* SONYA *are singing round the piano.* BORIS *is turning the pages for them.* PETYA *runs round, annoying them.*

The COUNT *and* COUNTESS *greet their guests.* PIERRE *enters and stands in the middle of the room getting in everyone's way.*

COUNTESS. Look, there's Pierre Bezuhov. I wasn't sure if he would come, with his father being so ill.

COUNT. I wasn't sure if he would come after that business in St. Petersburg. Dear oh dear!

COUNTESS. What do you mean?

COUNT. Apparently he and Anatole Kuragin and a certain young man named Dolohov, went rampaging through the streets with a bear. When the police tried to intervene, they tied a policeman to the back of the beast and threw them into the Neva. Can you imagine? (*He imitates this.*)

COUNTESS. Really! I hardly think that's a laughing matter. (*She smiles all the same.*) And they do say that his father has written to the Tsar, asking that Pierre be declared legitimate. He may be the next Count. Think of it – forty thousand serfs and millions of roubles.

MARIA DMITRIEVNA *enters.*

MARIA D. (*loudly*). Health and happiness to our dear one whose name-day it is.

COUNT. Ah, now the dancing can really begin!

NATASHA *breaks off from her song and comes running over*.

NATASHA. Maria Dmitrievna!

MARIA D. Well, and how's my Cossack? I suppose you think I have something for you.

NATASHA. I know you have.

COUNTESS. Natasha!

MARIA D. Here then. What do you say to these?

She hands her a pair of sparkling ear-rings. NATASHA *coos*.

NATASHA. Ooo, they're beautiful. Thank you. (*She kisses her and runs to show* SONYA.) Sonya, look.

MARIA D. She's a scamp of a girl but I'm fond of her all the same. (*She spies* PIERRE.) Ho, ho, sir! Come here to me.

PIERRE. Me?

MARIA D. Yes, you sir. Come along, come along. I was the only person to tell your father the truth when he was in high favour, and in your case it's a sacred duty. (*Pause. All hold their breath*.) A pretty fellow, I must say! A pretty fellow! His father lies on his death-bed and he amuses himself setting a policeman astride a bear! For shame, sir, for shame! It would be better if you went to the war.

She turns and offers her arm to the COUNT *who, stifling his laughter, escorts her away*.

NATASHA. How funny that fat Pierre is. I'm going to ask him to dance.

SONYA. Natasha, you can't.

PETYA. You wouldn't dare.

NATASHA. Yes I would. (*She strides across the room to* PIERRE.) Will you dance with me, Monsieur Bear? I mean Monsieur Pierre?

PIERRE. Oh, er . . . I don't dance . . . I'm afraid of spoiling the figures. (*but there is something in* NATASHA'*s warm, mischievous gaze that he cannot resist*.) But if you will be my teacher . . .

He stoops and offers her his arm and leads her to the floor. She looks back in delight at SONYA *and* PETYA *who are creased up with laughter*.

COUNTESS. Oh my goodness! Natasha, what are you doing?

NATASHA. What's the matter, Mama? Why shouldn't I?

They begin to dance. Other couples take to the floor, including the COUNT *and* MARIA DMITRIEVNA. *After several moments, the* ATTENDANT *crosses to* PIERRE *and whispers something in his ear.* PIERRE *bows to* NATASHA *and leaves.*

Scene 5

ANDREI's *room. Bald Hills.*

ANDREI *is finishing his packing. He is depressed and confused about his feelings at going away.* MARIA *enters. He assumes his usual impenetrable expression.*

MARIA. Must you go tonight, Andrusha?

ANDREI. Yes.

MARIA. Can I stay for a while?

ANDREI. Of course.

Pause. He goes on with his packing.

MARIA. What a treasure of a wife you have. She is like a child, a sweet merry-hearted child.

ANDREI. Ah. I take it you have been talked to.

She blushes. Pause.

MARIA. One must be indulgent to little weaknesses. Who is free from them?

ANDREI. I have no fault to find with my wife, Masha, no cause for self-reproach in regard to her. But ask me whether we are happy, the answer is no.

MARIA. 'Tout comprendre, c'est tout pardonner'. We must try to put ourselves in other people's places. She was brought up in society and now she is to part from her husband so soon, be left alone in the country . . .

ANDREI. You live in the country and don't find the life so terrible.

MARIA. But that's different. I have always been a solitary creature and am now, more so than ever. To be honest I don't even need Mlle Bourienne.

ANDREI. I don't like your Mlle Bourienne.

MARIA. Oh, she is very kind and good. I'm sure Lise will enjoy her company.

ANDREI. Yes. I'm sure she will.

MARIA (*reproachfully.*) Andrei, if you had faith you would have turned to God and implored Him to give you the love you do not feel.

ANDREI. Tell me the truth, Maria: I think Father's temper must make things very trying for you sometimes. He has always been harsh and now I should think he's getting extremely difficult.

Pause.

MARIA. You are a good man, except for a sort of intellectual pride. And pride is a great sin. Have we any right to judge Father? And even if we did, what feeling but vénèration could my father inspire? I am so contented with him. I only wish that you were all as happy as I am. (ANDREI *shakes his head incredulously.*) Andrei, we mustn't argue. Who knows when I will see you again. I have a great favour to ask of you.

ANDREI. What is it, my dear?

MARIA (*she takes a tiny icon from her reticule*). Our Grandfather wore it in all the battles he fought. Please, for my sake, wear this icon, and promise me never to take it off.

ANDREI. If it doesn't weigh half a hundredweight and won't break my neck. (*Seeing her serious face.*) I shall be glad to, my dear Maria. Very glad.

MARIA. 'He will save you in spite of yourself, and have mercy on you and bring you to Himself, for in Him alone is truth and peace.'

She crosses herself, kisses the icon and puts it around his neck. ANDREI crosses himself and kisses it.

The sounds of the war are heard growing louder from here to the end of the act.

Scene 6

COUNT BEZUHOV's *bed-chamber. The* BEZUHOV *house. Moscow.*

In the middle of the room is a huge bed surrounded by mourners and priests, performing their office with slow solemnity.

The majestic form of the COUNT *can just be seen emerging above the heavy quilt. In each of his hands, a lighted taper has been placed and the* ATTENDANT *and another servant kneel and hold them upright. The priests are chanting from the scriptures in their deep, bass voices.*

PIERRE *and* PRINCE VASILI *enter and pause in the doorway.*

VASILI. Courage, courage, mon ami. Your father has asked to see you. C'est bien.

He leads him forward. All make way for PIERRE *with a reverence he has never known before. He is given a lighted taper and confusedly tries to cross himself with the same hand. A woman sniggers.*

The priests come to the end of the rite and all leave with the exception of PIERRE *and the* ATTENDANT, *who sits in his corner.*

VASILI (*as he goes*). I know you must have much you wish to say to him.

Alone, PIERRE *wonders what he is supposed to do. He goes nearer to his father and looks at him. The old man's face begins to twitch and he utters a hoarse unintelligible sound.* PIERRE *panics – what does he want?*

PIERRE. Is it . . . you want to speak to me? You want Prince Vasili? A priest? You want a priest?

ATTENDANT. Wants to be turned over on the other side, the master does. Wants turning, that's all.

Between them they turn him. One of his arms flops about heavily. PIERRE *is dismayed. The old man smiles feebly. Tears start to* PIERRE's *eyes. He sits on a chair beside the bed with his head in his hands.*

Whilst this is happening, the ROSTOVs *enter and begin saying their long goodbyes to* NIKOLAI.

The BOLKONSKYS *enter and take leave of* ANDREI. LISA *swoons and is helped to a chair.* MARIA *takes his hand silently.*

The old PRINCE *enters and stands to one side.* ANDREI *goes to him.*

PRINCE B. You're off then. Kiss me here. (ANDREI *kisses him on the cheek.*) Thank you, Thank you.

ANDREI. Father, about my wife: when the time comes, will you send to Moscow for a doctor. She's afraid.

PRINCE B. It's a bad business, eh?

ANDREI. What is?

PRINCE B. You know what. But there's nothing to be done. There's no getting unmarried.

ANDREI. If anything were to happen to me and I have a son, keep him here with you.

PRINCE B. Not let your wife have him? (*He laughs.*) I see. I see. (*Hands him a letter.*) Give this to Mihail Kutuzov. See he treats you well. Remember, Prince Andrei: if you were killed, it would be a grief to me in my old age. Well, you have said goodbye, now go. Go!

PIERRE *has fallen asleep beside the bed.* PRINCE VASILI *and the* ATTENDANT *draw near.* VASILI *wakes* PIERRE.

VASILI. He has gone. Have no fear, dear boy. There will be trying times ahead, but I beg you to leave everything in my hands. I will take care of everything.

NATASHA *hugs* NIKOLAI *one last time.*

The sounds of the war fill the stage. ANDREI, *and* NIKOLAI *begin to go through some of the gestures of battle but they are held and restrained by those around them. Then they collapse down and are supported by those around them.*

The scene is disturbing and full of hope and grief.

Act Three

Scene 1

ANNA PAVLOVNA's *drawing room. St. Petersburg.*

ANNA's *set are assembled for another soirée.* HÉLÈNE *is present, primed for what is about to happen.*

PIERRE *and* PRINCE VASILI *enter.*

ATTENDANT. Count Piotr Kirillovich Bezuhov and Prince Vasili Kuragin.

ANNA. Ah, mon cher Comte, you are back amongst us. How delightful.

VASILI. The Count had a great deal of business to settle in Moscow.

ANNA. Bien-sûr, I quite understand. May I offer my profound condolences, Count, on the death of your esteemed father.

PIERRE. Thank you.

VASILI. The Count has just been sworn in as a Gentleman of the Bed-chamber – a post I managed to secure for him.

ANNA. Indeed? Felicitations! And what does your new position entail?

PIERRE. Nothing at all, as far as I can tell.

ANNA. Charmant! Such honesty. Vasili, you must go and talk to the Prussian Ambassador. He witnessed the meeting between his sovereign and our august Emperor at Potsdam. The alliance is most gratifying, n'est-ce pas? (VASILI, *understanding her double entendre, goes.* PIERRE *tries to follow.*) I must confess I have other designs for you this evening, Count. My dear Hélène confided to me that she is longing to see you again.

PIERRE. To see me?

ANNA. So you must consent to spend just a little of your time with her. (*They look over towards her –* PIERRE *is amazed.*)

ANNA. Isn't she exquisite? What perfection of manner! With her at his side, even the most unworldly of men could not fail to occupy a brilliant position in society. But forgive me – I am getting carried away. I only wanted your opinion.

She leads him to HÉLÈNE, *who smiles her best smile for* PIERRE. PIERRE *is overwhelmed by his proximity to this goddess. He kisses her hand. They sit – one on either side of her.*

PIERRE. I hope you are well.

HÉLÈNE. Quite well, thank you.

PIERRE. I have been staying with your father a week now, but I haven't seen you.

HÉLÈNE. I have been away.

Pause.

ANNA. I hear you are having your Petersburg house redecorated.

PIERRE. Yes. My architect has suggested some changes.

ANNA. An excellent idea. But don't give up your quarters at Prince Vasili's. You are still so young and need someone to advise you. If you were to marry, of course, it would be a different matter.

PIERRE (*glancing at* HÉLÈNE *in alarm*). Yes. Quite.

ANNA. Tea?

PIERRE. Thank you.

ANNA *passes a cup across* HÉLÈNE, *though* PIERRE *was about to walk round and take it. He is forced to lean terribly close to her. Music. Time seems to stop. He can smell her perfume and feel her warmth and is acutely aware of the 'living charm' of her bosom. Her eyes meet his. He sits up straight. The music fades.*

ANNA. Well, I will leave you two in your little corner. I can see you are very snug here.

The soirée suddenly disappears and PIERRE *is in his room, lying on his sofa, trying to get to sleep. He sits up abruptly.* NAPOLEON *is sitting nearby.*

PIERRE. What have I done? Nothing. Have I?

HÉLÈNE *enters, like a vision and sits beside him.*

PIERRE. I picked up her reticule when she came to leave, I . . .

Music. He relives the moment when he leant across to take the tea-cup. Then again, except this time his arm brushes across her neck and the next time his lips accidentally meet her cheek. Throughout the scene, as the moment is replayed, his desire becomes more extreme and the contact more overtly sexual.

I . . . oh . . . What have I done? What have I done? I cannot link my name with hers.

NAPOLEON. Then don't.

PIERRE. It cannot be. She is stupid, I have always said so, and yet . . . and yet, why is she stupid? She doesn't say much but what she says is clear and simple. Yes! She is a splendid girl!

NAPOLEON. Is this what you want?

PIERRE. Yes. No. I don't know.

NAPOLEON. If you don't want it, stop it.

PIERRE. You're right. This happiness is not for me, it is for people who don't have what I have inside me. I am a revolutionary! I am a leader of men! Oh! 'Bonaparte . . . Bonaparte was free when he worked his way towards his goal . . . ' (*By now he is practically having sex with her.*) Oh, what am I doing? I am in the abyss. I must pull myself out. Where is my will-power?

NAPOLEON. Where indeed?

PIERRE. Can it be that I have . . . none?

We are suddenly back in ANNA PAVLOVNA's *drawing room. There are no guests this time, but* PIERRE *and* HÉLÈNE *are sitting side by side, very straight and formal. Silence.* ANNA PAVLOVNA *and* VASILI *enter and watch from a distance.*

ANNA (*whispering*). I believe I may congratulate you on the acquisition of an extremely wealthy son-in-law.

VASILI. You are too hasty. This is the third time this week he has had opportunity to declare himself. If he doesn't speak soon, I shall be forced to intervene.

PIERRE (*standing up*). Well, it is getting late.

PRINCE VASILI *coughs very loudly and gives* PIERRE *a stern look.* PIERRE *sits down again. Pause.*

PIERRE (*tentatively*). Have you enjoyed this evening?

HÉLÈNE. Thank you, yes. It has been one of the nicest I can remember.

Pause.

VASILI (*whispering*). Right, that's it. (*He strides across the room.*) Thank God! Thank God! I couldn't help but overhear. My dear boy . . . she will make you a good wife. My little girl . . . I am very, very pleased! God bless you both! (*He cries and embraces them both.*) Anna Pavlovna, come here, come here.

ANNA. What joy! What joy! I am delighted.

Embraces over, ANNA *and* VASILI *leave.*

PIERRE. Hélène . . . (*He cannot go on.*)

HÉLÈNE. Oh, take off your . . . those.

She points to his spectacles. He removes them and squints at her. He is about to kiss her hand but she intercepts his lips and presses them to her own, rather roughly.

PIERRE (*formally*). Je vous aime.

Scene 2

The drawing room. The ROSTOV *house. Moscow.*

COUNTESS ROSTOV *is reading aloud a letter from* NIKOLAI.
The COUNT, NATASHA, SONYA *and* PETYA *are gathered
round.*

COUNTESS. 'I am writing to you from Olmutz . . . '

> *We see* NIKOLAI *riding ferociously in his first charge. We see
> the alarm on his face when his horse falls from under him. We
> see him struggle to pick himself up and look about in confusion.
> We see a French soldier come towards him.*
>
> *We see him panic. He tries his pistol – it won't work. He throws
> it hopelessly at the Frenchman and runs like a hunted wolf. As
> his mother reads, he runs and runs and finally collapses on the
> ground, clutching his arm and sobbing.*
>
> *In contrast,* PETYA, *with a toy sword, acts the story as written.*

COUNTESS. 'You can't imagine the strange frenzy one experi-
    ences during a charge. As we lined the horses up and stood with
    sabres drawn, the waiting became unbearable. Then the captain
    rose in the saddle and cried out, 'God be with you lads –
    Charge' – and we all, all as one, broke into a gallop. What
    elation! And the cry of 'Hurrah' roaring in my ears! We ran
    into a hail of bullets. My horse, Rook, took a bullet in the head.

NATASHA. Oh no!

COUNTESS. I was thrown to the ground but managed to recover
    just in time to see a group of French running towards me. I shot
    at them with my pistol and they at me. Three of them fell. One
    of them reached me and swung at me with his rifle. My arm
    was broken . . . (*Forcing herself to go on.*) but I shot him to the
    ground and reached the cover of the trees, where our own
    sharp-shooters were waiting for me. It was after this that I was
    made an officer.

She is overcome. The COUNT *takes the letter and continues.*

COUNT. The battle of Schon-Graben was a great victory. They
    say there will be an even greater battle soon. For now, as I have
    said, we are camped near Olmutz . . .

NATASHA. Where's that?

COUNT. . . . where we have excellent provisions. I have even
    managed to spend some time with Boris Drubetskoy, who sends
    his respects – especially to Natasha. Please don't worry about
    my arm . . .

The COUNTESS *is sobbing now. The* COUNT *breaks off and,
dabbing a tear from his own eye, comforts her.* SONYA *runs to*

a corner where she spins round and round until her skirts puff out like a balloon.

NATASHA. Please don't cry, Maman. It's only a little wound and he's been made an officer.

COUNT. We must send some money for his new uniform.

COUNTESS. What nobility of soul! Not a word about his sufferings.

PETYA. What are you all crying about? I'm very, very glad that my brother has distinguished himself. I'd have killed a lot more of those Frenchies. They're beasts. I'd have killed so many there would have been a whole pile of them.

NATASHA. Shut up, Petya! (*She chases him off.*)

SONYA. He's an officer! And a wounded hero!

NATASHA. Sonya, if you close your eyes can you see Nikolai? I mean, see him as he really is?

SONYA. Yes, of course.

NATASHA. Because I can't see Boris. I know what he's like but . . . (*She closes her eyes.*) . . . there's nothing.

SONYA. Oh, Natasha. Natasha, have you stopped loving Boris?

NATASHA. Yes. I think I have.

Scene 3

MARIA's *room. Bald Hills.*

MARIA *is sitting still, her face a picture of misery, as* LISA *puts the finishing touches to her new hair-style.*

LISA. This may be the turning-point of your life. There'll be no need for you to 'come out' when suitors are flocking here of their own accord.

MLLE BOURIENNE *enters in a state of great excitement.*

MLLE BOURIENNE. They're here! They're waiting in the drawing room. The son is very handsome. He has jet-black hair. He flew up the stairs like an eagle.

LISA (*standing* MARIA *up*). What do you think, Amelie?

MLLE BOURIENNE. Oh yes . . . chère Princesse you look . . . well, it is lovely. Lovely.

LISA. No, it's true. There's something not quite right. It must be the sash. The old one was better. Change it back, Marie.

MLLE BOURIENNE. Perhaps the coiffure is a little . . .

LISA. It's the sash. Trust me, Amelie. Marie, you must hurry.

MARIA *hasn't moved. She is on the verge of tears.*

MLLE BOURIENNE. Come, chère Princesse, just one more little effort.

MARIA. Leave me alone.

LISA. Well then, let me alter your coiffure. If I . . .

MARIA. Leave me alone, please. I don't care about any of it.

They realise she is in earnest and leave.

LISA (*from door*). But you will change the sash, won't you?

Receiving no reply, she goes. Alone, MARIA is almost hysterical with fear.

Why did they have to come here? Why couldn't Father just send them away? Why does everyone assume I am so desperate that I . . . I don't even want to marry.

Her imaginary man has entered the room and approaches her.

How am I supposed to go into the drawing room now? Even if I liked him, I could never be natural with him.

He touches her and she relaxes into his embrace. For a few moments she is lost in her fantasy.

No. It is impossible. I am too ugly.

MLLE B. *knocks on the door. The man disappears.*

MLLE B. (*with urgency*). Princesse? Princesse!

MARIA (*kneeling suddenly*). 'Desire nothing for myself, seek nothing. Man's future and thy destiny too, must remain hidden from thee.' Oh Lord, help me to be ready for whatever may come. I want nothing, nothing but to obey your will.

Scene 4

The drawing room. Bald Hills.

MARIA *takes a deep breath and enters.* LISA, MLLE BOURIENNE, PRINCE VASILI *and* ANATOLE *are engaged in a lively conversation. They fall silent. The men stand.*

LISA. Voilà Marie.

There is a pause as they take her in.

VASILI (*kissing her hand*). I am honoured to see you again, chère Princesse. I met you once as a child and loved you as a daughter. You probably do not remember.

MARIA. On the contrary, I remember you well.

VASILI. May I present to you my son, Anatole.

ANATOLE *bows to her, uninterestedly.* MARIA *cannot look.*

LISA. Prince Vasili and I are old friends, aren't we?

VASILI. Indeed.

LISA (*to* ANATOLE). Why were you never at Annette's? Ah, but I know. I have heard all about your little misdemeanours. I know about your pranks in Paris too. Tut tut!

MLLE BOURIENNE. What did you think of Paris? It is my home town.

ANATOLE (*smiling at her in an over-intimate way*). I liked it very much. Very much.

PRINCE BOLKONSKY *enters. He looks at* MARIA *disdainfully.*

PRINCE B. Well, how d'ye do, how d'ye do, glad to see you.

VASILI. Friendship laughs at distance, mon Prince. This is my son, Anatole.

PRINCE B. A fine young fellow. Come here then and let us get better acquainted. What's your name?

ANATOLE (*grinning*). Anatole.

PRINCE B. So tell me, what's happening in the war? Squaring up to Napoleon at Austerlitz, are we?

ANATOLE. I'm not sure . . .

PRINCE B. Not sure, eh? Well we are. Had a letter from Prince Andrei. There's going to be a battle. A decisive battle. You're serving in the Horse Guards, are you not?

ANATOLE. Yes, but . . .

PRINCE B. Excellent. So you've been ordered to the front.

ANATOLE. No Prince. Our regiment has gone to the front but I am attached to . . . er, what is it I'm attached to, Papa?

PRINCE B. Ha! A credit to the service, I must say. 'What is it I'm attached to?' Ha ha. (ANATOLE *laughs too. The* PRINCE *suddenly frowns.*) Well, you may go. (*Turning on* MARIA.) Nice, very nice. You have got yourself up like that for visitors and before visitors I tell you, never dare in future to change your style of dressing without my consent.

Pause.

LISA. It was my fault, mon père . . .

PRINCE B. You, madam, may do as you please, but she need not make a scarecrow of herself, she's plain enough as it is.

MARIA. *begins to cry, silently. The clock strikes eight.*

Ah, dinner. Shall we?

ANATOLE *goes to take* MLLE. BOURIENNE's *arm. The* PRINCE *notices the look passed between them before* PRINCE VASILI *shoves his son in the direction of* MARIA.

ANATOLE *stops in front of her.* MARIE *looks up and into his eyes. Music.* ANATOLE *offers her his hand, smiling. She takes it. He kisses her hand. She feels that her fantasy is coming true. She perceives him as a kind and wonderful being.*

Scene 5

PRINCE BOLKONSKY's *study. Bald Hills.*

MARIA *stands before her father, full of hope.*

PRINCE B. Prince Vasili finds you to his taste as a daughter-in-law and makes you a proposal for his protégé. I wish to know your answer.

MARIA. But I do not know what you think, mon père.

PRINCE B. I? I? It's not me he wants to marry. It is your opinion I should be glad to learn. (*Pause.*)

MARIA. I only want to carry out your wishes . . . but if I had to express my own desires . . .

PRINCE B. Admirable! Capital! He will take you with your dowry and take your Mlle Bourienne into the bargain. She'll be the wife to him, while you . . .

MARIA. Father, what are you saying? What do you mean?

PRINCE B. (*seeing she is almost in tears*). Now, now, nothing at all. Just my little joke, you know. I hold to the principle, princess, that a girl has a perfect right to choose. Go to bed now and think it over. Come to me in the morning, and tell me your decision – yea or nay. Pray over it, if you must, but you would do better to exercise your judgement. Now go.

She leaves.

(*Shouting after her.*) Yea or nay. Yea or nay.

Scene 6

The chapel. Bald Hills.

MARIA *is beside herself with excitement.*

MARIA. Is he really to be my husband, this handsome stranger who is so kind? Yes, above all he is kind. And gentle. The way he looked at me, the way he took my hand . . . If it is Your will to impose on me the duties of wife and mother, I shall endeavour to fulfil them as faithfully as I am able.

She hears familiar voices giggling and whispering outside her door.

Who's there?

She goes to the door and looks out. MLLE BOURIENNE *and* ANATOLE *are standing in the corridor in a passionate embrace.* ANATOLE *looks round and sees* MARIA. MLLE. BOURIENNE *sees her and, uttering a little scream, runs away.* ANATOLE *bows to* MARIA *with an amused smile, as though inviting her to share the joke. He shrugs and walks off.*

Scene 7

PRINCE BOLKONSKY's *study. Bald Hills.*

MARIA *stands before* PRINCE BOLKONSKY, PRINCE VASILI *and* ANATOLE.

MARIA. I do not wish to marry. My desire, mon père, is never to leave you or part my life from yours.

PRINCE B. (*beside himself with joy*). Nonsense! Stuff and nonsense! (*He squeezes her hand tightly.*)

VASILI. My dear, can you give us no hope of touching your heart, which is so generous? Say that perhaps . . .

MARIA. What I have told you is all my heart can say. I thank you for the honour but I shall never be your son's wife.

Pause.

PRINCE B. Well, that's the end of that then. Very glad to have seen you, dear fellow, very glad. Go back to your room now, Princess. Go along.

She leaves. MLLE BOURIENNE *rushes to her.*

MLLE BOURIENNE. Oh, Princesse, I have lost your affection forever.

MARIA. No. I love you more than before.

MLLE BOURIENNE. You, who are so pure, could never understand being swept away by passion.

MARIA. I understand everything. I know how much you must love him to so far forget yourself. I will do all I can to bring about a match between you. Now leave me. (*She does so.*) Oh Andrei, where are you now? Where are you?

We see ANDREI *with the standard on the battle field at Austerlitz. We see him fall, and a terrible dark silence descends. After a few moments, a French soldier approaches him, tugs the icon from around his neck, and leaves.*

Scene 8

The drawing room. The BEZUHOV *house. Moscow.*

PIERRE *is sitting in semi-darkness. His dapper appearance is at odds with his gloomy countenance. He is very still and has been in the same position for an hour. After a moment he picks up a letter which is lying in his lap, and reads it with familiarity, as if trying to make new sense of it.*

PIERRE. 'Count, your spectacles are of no use. Your wife's intimacy with Dolohov is a secret to no-one but yourself. Open your eyes. A well-wisher.'

HÉLÈNE *enters. She is preparing to go out.*

HÉLÈNE. What's the matter with you?

PIERRE. Nothing. (*He crumples the note in his hand.*)

HÉLÈNE. What are you dressed up like that for?

PIERRE. I'm going to the English Club. There's a banquet for the heroes of Austerlitz.

HÉLÈNE. It's really rather ridiculous when you think about it: we suffer our greatest defeat in living memory and yet the men at the English Club still have to have their celebratory dinner.

PIERRE. The army can't be blamed for the defeat. I mean, from all accounts they acquitted themselves heroically. Bagration's men especially were . . .

HÉLÈNE. What would you know about it? You've never handled a weapon in your life. In fact, I can't imagine why you are going to the club. It will be elderly diplomats at one end and famous young officers at the other.

PIERRE. Like Dolohov.

HÉLÈNE. Yes. Like Dolohov. You will be an absurd misfit, comme toujours. (*She starts to go.*)

PIERRE. It's strange that Dolohov has followed us here from St. Petersburg.

HÉLÈNE. What's strange about it? If you're fool enough to give him the run of your houses, what do you expect? I'm surprised half of Russia hasn't moved in. I'm going out.

She leaves. PIERRE *stays still. The sights and sounds of the English Club begin to fill the stage around him. There are men in uniform and some in tail-coats, all drinking and laughing and talking. No-one approaches* PIERRE, *though occasionally someone bows to him.* COUNT ROSTOV, *who has organised the dinner, moves from group to group, slapping backs and spreading good cheer.*

DOLOHOV, NIKOLAI *and* ANATOLE *enter. They are clearly an established clique.* PIERRE *is acutely aware of* DOLOHOV.

DOLOHOV. I'll tell you why we lost: we lost because we were trampled underfoot by the fleeing Austrians.

NIKOLAI (*apprehending the* COUNT). Father, you must meet this man. This is Dolohov – the one I told you about who led his men across the ice.

COUNT. So, you've been playing the hero together out there. Excellent, excellent. You must come and visit us. (*He notices* PIERRE *and goes to him.*) Ah, Pierre. Very glad to see you here. I wanted a chance to thank you for those pineapples. Your hot-houses were my only hope. We've put them to good use as you shall see.

PIERRE. Yes. Thank you.

COUNT. Enjoying yourself, I hope?

PIERRE. Yes.

COUNT. Excellent. Nikolai is here. He's an officer now, you know. (*Noticing* PIERRE's *gloom.*) Are you sure you're all right? (PIERRE *nods.*) I was sorry to hear about Andrei Bolkonsky. Friend of yours, wasn't he?

PIERRE. Yes.

COUNT. Terrible thing that – missing in action. Better to know one way or the other. I pity his father. Ah, that's the Prince arriving. Have a drink, old boy.

He goes. There is a burst of laughter from DOLOHOV's *group.*

NIKOLAI. No, I am not 'in love' with him. But I love him as every man should love his emperor.

ANATOLE. I do believe there are tears in his eyes.

NIKOLAI. I saw him after Austerlitz. Bagration sent me with a message. By the time I found him it was all over. He was sitting alone. He was weeping. He really cares.

DOLOHOV. He does care. You're right.

ANATOLE. Let's drink – To the health of our sovereign the Emperor!

All raise their glasses. Everyone seated, stands, with the exception of PIERRE.

NIKOLAI (*to* PIERRE). What's the matter with you? It's a toast to the health of his Majesty.

PIERRE. *stands, reluctantly. All cry 'Hurrah!' and* ROSTOV *is the first to smash his glass on the ground.*

PIERRE (*as the noise subsides*). I'm sorry, Nikolai. How are you?

NIKOLAI *chooses not to hear and turns away.*

DOLOHOV. Aren't you going to renew the acquaintance?

NIKOLAI. Forget him. He's a fool.

DOLOHOV. One should always be civil to the husbands of pretty women. (*Loudly.*) Now I propose a toast. (*He approaches* PIERRE.) Here's to the health of all lovely women, Peterkins. And their lovers.

PIERRE *stands up, suddenly unable to control himself.*

PIERRE. How dare you? (DOLOHOV *looks him straight in the eye and drinks.*) You . . . you . . . blackguard! (*He grabs the glass from* DOLOHOV *and hurls it to the ground.*) I challenge you.

DOLOHOV *begins to laugh.*

ANATOLE. Come now, gentleman, there's no need for this. Shake hands and it will all be . . .

PIERRE. I don't want to shake hands. I challenge you to a duel.

He storms out.

Scene 9

PRINCE BOLKONSKY's *study. Bald Hills.*

The PRINCE *is working at his lathe.* MARIA *enters.*

PRINCE B. Ah, Princess Maria.

MARIA *realises he is choking back tears.*

MARIA. Father? It is Andrei . . .

He throws down his chisel. The wheel continues to turn.

PRINCE B. A letter has come from Kutuzov. He writes that he saw Andrei fall. He is killed!

MARIA. But, Father . . .

PRINCE B. Scoundrels! Blackguards! Destroying the army! Destroying men! And for what?

MARIA (*starting to cry*). But surely there is hope? While there is no body . . .

PRINCE B. I have had a man out there searching for a month. There is nothing. Kutuzov has found nothing. He is killed.

(MARIA *sees the letter, takes it and reads.*) PIERRE *and*
NAPOLEON *enter at one side of the stage and* DOLOHOV
and NIKOLAI *at the other.* NIKOLAI *walks forward and
places a marker in the middle, then goes back to* DOLOHOV.

NAPOLEON *and* NIKOLAI – *the two seconds* – *hand guns to
the adversaries.* NAPOLEON *shows* PIERRE *how to fire.*

NIKOLAI *gives a signal and* DOLOHOV *and* PIERRE *begin
to advance slowly towards the marker.* DOLOHOV *holds his
arm steady.* PIERRE *stumbles all over the place. Suddenly*
PIERRE *fires.* DOLOHOV *is hit. He slumps and pauses, then
drags himself forward.* PIERRE *dashes towards him.*

DOLOHOV. No! No, it's not over. (*He raises his gun.*)

NIKOLAI. Stand sideways, Pierre. Cover yourself!

DOLOHOV *fires and misses. He lets out an agonised groan.*

PIERRE *drops his gun and puts his hands to his head.*
NAPOLEON *goes to him and begins to congratulate him.*

PIERRE. Go! Leave me! (*He staggers off.*)

PRINCE B. The finest men in Russia led out to slaughter. Waste!
A horrible waste!

MARIA (*taking her father's hand*). Father, let us weep together.
(*He turns away.*)

PRINCE B. Go! Go and tell Lisa he is dead. Go!

PRINCE B. *and the participants in the duel, leave.* LISA
*enters. She is very big now. She sits in a chair doing her
embroidery.* MARIA *goes to her. She smiles.*

LISA. Marie, give me your hand. (*She places* MARIA's *hand on
her belly.*) There – there – can you feel it? It feels so strange.
You know, I am going to love him very much. (MARIA *begins
to cry.*) What is it, Masha?

MARIA. Nothing. I just felt sad . . . about Andrei.

LISA. Is there news?

MARIA. No. No news.

They remain on stage through the next scene.

Scene 10

PIERRE's *room. The* BEZUHOV *house. Moscow.*

PIERRE *enters. He is in utter despair. He slumps down on the
sofa.* NAPOLEON *enters and paces the room.*

NAPOLEON. What is the matter with you? You have done what you always dreamt of – you decided on a course of action and you carried it through.

PIERRE. It was pointless.

NAPOLEON. You defended your honour and the honour of the woman you love.

PIERRE. I don't love her.

NAPOLEON. A figure of speech.

PIERRE. Even as I pulled the trigger I knew it was a sham. He was not to blame. Wouldn't I, any man, have done the same thing in his position? My wife is a dissolute woman. I always knew it but I pretended not to because . . . because I desired her. But even on the first night I gratified that desire, it made me sick. Do you know, there was even talk of a liaison between her and her brother? I knew that and yet I married her. (*Pause.*) She refuses to let me touch her. Have you any idea how that feels?

NAPOLEON. It is not a problem I have ever encountered.

PIERRE. She once told me she would rather die than bear me children. She despises me that much. And I despise her. So don't talk to me about honour.

HÉLÈNE *enters and paces the room like a cat before striking.*

HÉLÈNE. Setting yourself up as a hero now, are you? What did you mean to prove? I'm asking you a question. You believe everything you are told. You are like some kind of ridiculous child. I'll tell you what you have proved with your duel: you have proved what everyone in Moscow already thought – that you are a fool. And you have made me a laughing stock.

PIERRE. Is he dead?

HÉLÈNE. What if he were?

PIERRE (*quietly.*) Then he's not.

HÉLÈNE. Do you want to know what people are saying? They are saying you were drunk and needlessly challenged a man you are jealous of, a man who's superior to you in every way. (*An awful feeling of agony is rising in* PIERRE.) And what made you think I was his lover? Well? Because I like his company? If you were more intelligent and normal, I should have preferred yours.

PIERRE. Don't speak to me, I beg you.

HÉLÈNE. There are not many wives with husbands like you who would not have taken lovers. I have not done so.

PIERRE. We had better part.

HÉLÈNE. By all means, on condition you provide for me. Part? Ha! There's a threat to frighten me with!

PIERRE (*springing up and rushing at her*). I'll kill you!

He seizes a slab of marble from the table and smashes it at her feet. She shrieks in terror.

(*Roaring.*) Get out!

HÉLÈNE *runs from the room*. LISA *suddenly groans in pain*.

LISA. It is only indigestion . . . oh, Mon Dieu! Say it is only indigestion, say so Marie . . . oh . . .

MARIA. I'll get help. (*She runs off.*)

LISA. Don't leave me. I don't want it to happen! I don't want it to happen.

Scene 11

A post station waiting room, between Moscow and St. Petersburg. An elderly man (BAZDEYEV) is sitting near the fire, drinking tea. There is something impressive about him – he seems calm and at peace. PIERRE enters. It is a freezing night but he seems oblivious to the cold and everything else. The ATTENDANT enters and gives him some tea.

ATTENDANT. The post-master says there should be some horses in a couple of hours, sir. If not, he'll let us have the horses reserved for the mail. We'll soon be on our way.

PIERRE. Whatever.

The ATTENDANT leaves. Pause.

BAZDEYEV. I have the pleasure of addressing Count Bezuhov, if I am not mistaken.

PIERRE (*blushing uneasily*). Yes.

BAZDEYEV. I belong to the Brotherhood of Freemasons, and in their name and my own I hold out a brotherly hand to you. If for any reason you feel averse from talking to me . . .

PIERRE. Not at all. On the contrary. But I'm afraid . . . how shall I put it? My way of thinking in regard to the whole universe is so opposed to yours that I'm afraid we shall not understand one another. I don't believe in God.

BAZDEYEV. Yes, you do not know Him. You cannot know Him and that is why you are unhappy.

PIERRE (*startled*). I am unhappy. (*Pause.*) I keep asking myself, what is life for and what am I? And there is no answer. I used to think that my life meant something. Like Napoleon, I thought

I would find something to fight for, but there is nothing. We live and then we die. I shot someone – in a duel.

BAZDEYEV. Yes. I have heard of your misfortune.

PIERRE. I hate my life. I hate it.

BAZDEYEV. Examine your actions to date: you have become the possessor of great wealth; how have you used it? What have you done for your fellow men? What have you done for your tens of thousands of serfs? Have you tried to help them, physically or morally? No. You have profited by their toil to lead a dissipated life. You married, took upon yourself the responsibility of guiding a young woman through life but did you help her to find the path of truth? No, you flung her into an abyss of deceit. You say you do not know God, but let me tell you, He is here. He exists, but to understand Him is hard.

PIERRE. Please explain to me. If He exists, why can't we know it? Why can't he make us certain?

BAZDEYEV. Supreme wisdom may be compared to the purest dew. Whilst my soul is an impure vessel, I cannot imbibe this dew.

PIERRE. Yes I see that.

BAZDEYEV. First I must bring the dew already contained within myself to some degree of purity and to do this God has implanted the divine light called conscience in our souls. Turn thy spiritual gaze into thine inmost being. Purify thyself and as thou art purified thou wilt gain wisdom. (*He stands and prepares to leave.*) Where are you going to, sir?

PIERRE. St. Petersburg. I have left my wife. Sir, please don't think me altogether bad. With my whole soul I have wished that I were what you would have me be. But I have never met with any help from anyone. Help me. Teach me and someday perhaps . . . (*He cannot go on.*)

BAZDEYEV. Go to Petersburg. Devote some time to solitude and self-examination. Read Thomas à Kempis. We will contact you.

He leaves. PIERRE *recovers himself.*

PIERRE (*to* ATTENDANT). Who was that man?

ATTENDANT. His name is Osip Alexeyevich Bazdeyev, sir.

PIERRE (*quietly*). Thank you. Thank you.

Scene 12

The drawing room. Bald Hills.

Princess MARIA *is trying to pray, but is too agitated and gives up.* MLLE BOURIENNE *and the* ATTENDANT *are with her.*

MARIA. This is unbearable. Why doesn't the doctor come? How long can it take him to get from Moscow?

MLLE BOURIENNE. It is a dreadful night.

MARIA. What if he's lost?

ATTENDANT. The Prince has sent men to the high-road to guide him through the snow. Don't fret, Miss. The midwife is with her. I remember when your poor dear mother was brought to bed of you, in Kishinyov, with only a peasant woman to help. It's all in God's hands.

He goes.

MLLE BOURIENNE. Princesse, there's people driving up the avenue. With lanterns. It must be the doctor.

MARIA. Thank God.

MARIA *runs to the hallway. There is a man there, standing with his back to her, shaking snow from his hat. He turns.*

MARIA. Andrei! Oh Lord, it cannot be. It cannot be! (*He comes to her and embraces her.*) Andrei . . .

ANDREI. You didn't get my letter? (*She cannot answer.*) Dear Masha . . . (*He hugs her again.*) Dear Masha. Where is she? Has the baby come yet?

MARIA. No. Hurry, you must go to her. Hurry.

ANDREI *leaves.* MARIA *is overwhelmed by this seeming miracle.*

PRINCE BOLKONSKY *enters.*

PRINCE B (*quietly.*) Is it true?

MARIA (*embracing him*). Oh, my father . . . it is true. God has brought him back to us.

After a few moments the ATTENDANT *enters. The expression on his face warns them that all is not well.*

ATTENDANT. Your excellency . . . a son.

MARIA. And Lisa?

The ATTENDANT *shakes his head.* ANDREI *returns. He doesn't look at them. They watch as he wanders into the room.*

ANDREI. I thought of her, the night before Austerlitz . . . and when I was injured . . . I remembered the first time we met. I remembered my love for her. I thought of our child growing inside her and . . . I wished I had been kinder.

PRINCE BOLKONSKY *goes to him and, throwing his arms tightly round* ANDREI'*s neck, sobs like a child.*

Act Four

Scene 1

Almost three years have passed.

Music. Images – PIERRE taking HÉLÈNE's hand in formal reconciliation. They kiss – as they did on their betrothal.

MARIA fastens the buttons of three-year-old NIKOLAI's jacket, and smoothes his hair. She kisses him.

As she does so, lights come up on ANDREI, sad and alone. MARIA sends NIKOLAI over to him, but he looks at him as if he is a stranger and the boy runs back to his aunt.

NATASHA and SONYA, now in long skirts with their hair up, and PETYA, now a robust thirteen-year-old, gather round the piano to sing. NIKOLAI passes through.

SONYA. Nikolai? Will you come and sing with us?

NIKOLAI (*coldly*). I haven't time. I'm going to the club.

He leaves. SONYA looks dejected but rejoins the others. As they sing a bright and happy song, we see NIKOLAI sitting down to play cards with DOLOHOV. NIKOLAI starts to lose. The happier their song becomes, the more he loses and the more abject he becomes. As they come to the end and laugh, NIKOLAI is bankrupt and leaves in despair.

Scene 2

The drawing room. The ROSTOV house. St. Petersburg.

NIKOLAI, SONYA, and the COUNTESS are sitting in the drawing room with BORIS DRUBETSKOY who is now a chic aide-de-camp.

NATASHA almost runs in but then stops and, straightening her dress and calming down, enters like a young lady.

COUNTESS. Well Boris, do you recognize your playmate of old?

BORIS (*rising in astonishment and kissing NATASHA's hand*). I can hardly believe the change in you, Natasha. You have grown so lovely.

NATASHA. I should hope so! And does Mama look older?

COUNTESS. You see, in reality she has hardly changed at all.

BORIS. On the contrary, the Countess looks younger than ever, and more beautiful.

COUNTESS (*laughing*). Really!

NATASHA. But it's years since we saw you. We thought you had forgotten us.

COUNTESS. Of course he hadn't forgotten us.

BORIS. A great deal has happened in those four years, has it not, Nikolai?

NIKOLAI. Oh yes, a great deal.

BORIS. And then, you are so rarely in St. Petersburg.

COUNTESS. Well now that we are here, you must visit often.

> NATASHA *has sat down and is studying her childhood suitor. He feels the weight of her scrutiny and is unnerved.*
>
> Boris is adjutant to Prince Dolgorukov, Natasha. He was just saying that he was actually present at Tilsit when the peace was signed. Could you see Napoleon?

BORIS. At one point the Emperor was no further from me than Nikolai is now.

COUNTESS. Indeed? What does he look like? Is he short?

BORIS. He is short, but I can honestly say, I never saw a man so impressive. His bearing and countenance emanate greatness.

COUNTESS. Really?

BORIS. Oh yes. (*Glancing at* NATASHA.) You know, the two emperors met in a pavilion, erected on rafts, anchored in the middle of the Niemen. It was an extraordinary spectacle and one I shall never forget. (*Again, at* NATASHA.) The interview lasted exactly one hour and fifty-three minutes. I know this because it was understood that I would take upon myself the task of noting down every fact of historic relevance.

COUNTESS. How thrilling. You must be terribly important.

BORIS. Not at all. But it is a role I believe I shall often be called upon to perform. Well, I'm afraid I must go. I am invited to a reception at Countess Bezuhov's.

COUNTESS. Ah, how is the 'Queen of Petersburg'?

BORIS. Very well. Though she will be most unhappy if I am even five minutes late. Natasha . . . (*Kisses her hand.*) Nikolai, how long are you on leave? Perhaps I will see you at the club.

NIKOLAI. Perhaps.

BORIS. I was sorry to hear of your misfortune last night. I'm sure your luck will turn.

The COUNTESS *and* BORIS *leave.*

NIKOLAI. Good God, what a pompous ass he is!

NATASHA. Nikolai!

NIKOLAI. They're all the same these adjutants, with their immaculate hair-dos and their kid gloves. Damned dandies! Put them in the thick of action and they're worse than useless. Taking notes at Tilsit! He's no more than a jumped-up scribe.

NATASHA. I had no idea you felt like that.

NIKOLAI. I went to him for help about a friend of mine a few months ago. I found him having dinner with some French officers. Well, I'm afraid we men at the sharp end can't be so quick to change our opinion of the French. It wasn't long ago we were cutting their throats and calling Bonaparte a criminal: now it's the 'Great Emperor Napoleon'. It makes me sick. You wouldn't think of taking up with him again, would you?

NATASHA. Why not? After all, we're still engaged.

NIKOLAI. I strongly advise you against it. He's a careerist. His name has been linked with several heiresses, not to mention Hélène Bezuhov.

NATASHA. All the more fun to make him fall in love with me. Oh, don't be angry with me, Nikolai, darling passionate Nikolai. I'm only teasing.

She leaves. SONYA *approaches* NIKOLAI, *but he turns away.*

NIKOLAI. Sometimes I wish we were still at war. I wish I was back with the regiment. It was all so straightforward. No decisions, no mess.

SONYA. Did you lose very badly last night?

NIKOLAI. I don't want to talk about it. You won't tell anyone what I said about the French, will you? If the Emperor thinks we should make allies of them it must be right to. It's hard, that's all.

Scene 3

PRINCE ANDREI'*s study. Bald Hills.*

ANDREI *is working. The* ATTENDANT *shows* PIERRE *to the door.* PIERRE *indicates silently that he should leave. He does so.*

PIERRE. Excuse me, sir. You have a visitor. (ANDREI *looks up.*) I hope I'm not interrupting.

ANDREI. No, no. Not at all.

He accepts PIERRE's *embrace, but is frowning.*

PIERRE. I thought I'd better come and find you, seeing as you never come to town anymore. You know, everyone has you down as a recluse.

ANDREI. I have no reason to come to town. So, how are you?

PIERRE. Very well, thank you. I've missed you. I've just got back from a tour of my estates, and I was thinking, 'Who is it I want to tell about all this?' And of course, it was you. It was wonderful, Andrei. I've taken steps to liberate my serfs.

ANDREI. Really?

PIERRE. Yes. And until that's completed, I've introduced a new labour system. The peasants work shorter hours. Women with young children don't work at all. I've abolished corporal punishment. I've set up alms-houses and schools on every estate. And hospitals. And it works! You could do . . .

ANDREI. Do the same here? I had a feeling that was coming.

PIERRE. You should have seen the welcome I got in the villages. The people! In one place they begged me to allow them to add a new chantry to the church in honour of my patron saints. At their own expense! It's the thought that I'm improving their spiritual well-being that gives me the most satisfaction. From now on they will learn the doctrines of a future life, one where they will find recompense and solace.

ANDREI. Ah. Your masonic precepts.

PIERRE. Yes. I want them to see beyond meaningless church ceremonies. All that Latin!

ANDREI. And what if they don't want their spiritual needs awakened?

PIERRE. What, sorry?

ANDREI. Has it ever occurred to you that their very happiness lies in their animal existence? Don't get me wrong, I envy them. That animal happiness is the only true kind, and you want to deprive them of it! Physical labour is as essential to the peasant as intellectual activity is for you or I. Stop him ploughing or mowing and he starts drinking or puts on weight and falls ill.

PIERRE. Of course. He can still be physically active, but he must have a spiritual life . . .

ANDREI. And then what happens at your hospitals? A peasant has a stroke and is dying but you have him patched up and he drags about, a cripple, for another ten years, a burden to everyone, not least himself. It would be simpler for him to die. Plenty of others are being born to take his place.

Pause.

PIERRE. Well . . . perhaps we should talk about this later.

ANDREI. No, let's talk about it now.

PIERRE. I can't believe you really think that. Explain to me: what, what exactly can be wrong in the peasant being educated? What can be the harm in a woman who has just given birth having proper care and . . .

ANDREI. 'Harm'. Now that's a difficult word. Surely only God can know what is harmful.

PIERRE. Harm? Harm? It's quite straightforward, we all know what harms us. To kill a man is harmful.

ANDREI. I know of only one real evil in life: remorse. To live for myself so as to avoid that evil: that is the sum of my wisdom now.

PIERRE. That's not enough. I lived for myself and I almost ruined my life.

ANDREI. You once asked me why I was going to war. Do you remember? The simple answer was that I wanted honour and glory. And what is glory but that same love for others, the desire to help, the desire for their praise? I not almost but totally ruined my life. Now I see all that for the sham it really is. I live for myself and my family and I have found peace. You must see Maria before you go. There's a person who lives for everyone but herself. Even now, she'll be in the chapel with her God's folk. And where does it get her?

PIERRE. So what do you intend to do? Live out here without engaging with anybody? Trying to avoid doing anything you might regret until the day you die?

ANDREI. Yes. Yes, that's exactly what I intend to do.

Scene 4

The garden. Bald Hills. The light is fading. The moon and stars are just visible. PIERRE *and* ANDREI *stand in silence before the shrine dedicated to* LISA, *in which she is depicted as an angel.*

PIERRE. Andrei, I must just say this: I know you think freemasonry is just a religious sect, but the more I learn of it, the more I realise that it is the one expression of the highest, of the eternal, in humanity.

ANDREI. There is nothing high about humanity. Humanity is base and wicked. (*He looks up at* LISA.) An Italian sculptor made this. I sent him her portrait. Do you know what's really amazing? He has captured the exact look on her face before she died: 'I love you all and have done no-one any harm; and what have you done to me?'

PIERRE. Do you believe in a future life? You're right: here on earth it is all lies and wickedness. But in the universe there is a kingdom of truth and we who are now the children of the earth are, in the eternal sense, part of that vast, harmonious whole. If I see clearly the ladder rising from plant to man, why should I suppose that it breaks off with me, and does not lead further, up to superior beings, the God-head? I cannot vanish. Nothing in this world ever vanishes. Above me, all around, there are spirits, and in their world, there is truth.

ANDREI. If only it were so.

They gaze up at the sky. In the chapel, MARIA is praying with her God's-folk. The pilgrims are a strange collection of people, in rags, with bare feet. One elderly woman – THEODOSIA – is wound about with chains.

MARIA approaches. She is embarrassed and disconcerted.

MARIA. Andrei, why didn't you let me know? (PIERRE *kisses her hand.*) I am very glad to see you.

THEODOSIA (*approaching*). Why aren't you going to the right place? Go to Kolyazin, there's a wonder-working icon revealed there. Drops of holy oil trickle down the cheeks of the Most Holy Mother of God.

ANDREI. I suppose you saw it with your own eyes?

THEODOSIA. Oh yes, master, I was found worthy – first one drop and then another.

PIERRE. You see, this is the way they impose on the people. It's a trick.

ANDREI. Of course it's trick.

THEODOSIA. Oh master, whatever are you saying? And you with a son. May God forgive you . . .

MARIA. That will do, Theodosia. (*She goes.*) Andrei, why do you torment them? Will you go to the nursery and say good-night to Nikolai. He was asking for you.

ANDREI. Very well. (*He kisses her and goes.*)

PIERRE. I truly did not mean to hurt her feelings, Princess. I understand them so well and have the greatest respect for them.

MARIA. You are very kind. They are all pilgrims. I encourage them to stop here. It is the one thing in which . . . my father doesn't like it. I hope you are happy. I heard of the trouble in your life . . .

PIERRE. My wife and I are reconciled. I know my duty now.

MARIA. I'm glad. But what do you think of Andrei? I am worried about him. Last Spring his wound re-opened and the doctor said he should go abroad for treatment but he wouldn't. And his state of mind frightens me. He's not the sort to weep away his grief. If you could only persuade him to go back to St. Petersburg with you. He needs life. Please try, Pierre.

Scene 5

The COUNTESS's *room. The* ROSTOV *house. St. Petersburg.*

NATASHA *and her mother are in bed.* NATASHA *is playing a game, kissing her mother's hand – first the knuckle, then the space in between.*

NATASHA. January, February, March, April . . .

COUNTESS. Boris is very nice and I love him like a son. But you are sixteen, Natasha. At your age I was already married. You must think seriously about what it is you want. You have completely turned his head, you must see that.

NATASHA. Do you really think so?

COUNTESS. But what do you want of him? You know you can't marry him.

NATASHA. Why not?

COUNTESS. Because he's poor. And I know you're not in love.

NATASHA. How do you know?

COUNTESS. I just do.

NATASHA. But if I want to marry him . . .

COUNTESS. No, it's not right, Natasha.

NATASHA. But if I choose to . . .

COUNTESS. No. You are so young, my darling. You will go to your first ball on New Year's Eve and you will soon see that there are plenty of attractive . . .

NATASHA. May, June, July, August . . . Do you think he is very much in love with me? Did anyone ever love you so much? But you're right, he isn't quite to my taste. He's narrow, like the dining-room clock. And pale coloured – pale gray. Bezuhov, now he's blue – dark blue and red and all square.

COUNTESS. You flirt with him, as well.

NATASHA. No I don't. We're just friends.

COUNTESS. I will talk to Boris tomorrow and tell him not to call so often.

NATASHA. What? Mama, don't you dare.

COUNTESS. I am quite decided.

NATASHA. All right, all right, I won't marry him, but we'll just go on as we are.

COUNTESS. What do you mean, my pet?

NATASHA. I mean, not get married . . . just go on as we are.

COUNTESS (*laughing*). 'As we are? As we are?' Oh Natasha, whatever made you think anyone can go on as they are?

NATASHA (*tickling her mother*). Don't laugh at me.

She runs to the ballroom and dances infront of the mirror, then sings in her operatic voice –

NATASHA. Isn't that Natasha Rostova? Yes, and isn't she exquisite? She's unusually intelligent, and she swims and she rides, and her voice! Well! One might even say a marvellous voice!

Scene 6

The New Year's Eve ball. St. Petersburg.

Guests fill the stage, including PIERRE and HÉLÈNE, ANDREI, ANNA PAVLOVNA, PRINCE VASILI, BORIS and ANATOLE. The host and hostess are greeting their guests. The ROSTOVS enter.

ATTENDANT. Count and Countess Rostov. Nikolai Rostov. Natasha Rostova. Sonya Rostova.

The women form one line and the men another in readiness for the dancing. Although genteel music plays, there is an increasingly military feel as the lines move back and then forward, culminating in something very like the charge. The couples pair off automatically and dance. NATASHA is left alone. Tears well in her eyes.

NATASHA. Can it be that no-one will approach me? They don't even see me. Please, oh please, let someone dance with me. (*She begins to dance on her own.*) I am Natasha Rostova. Don't you see how charming I am, how intelligent and pretty and graceful I am? And what a voice! One might say a marvellous voice!

PIERRE *notices her plight and intercepts* ANDREI.

PIERRE. I have a protégé here, the little Rostov girl. I said I would find her a partner. Do go and ask her.

ANDREI. Which is she?

PIERRE. There – in the white dress.

ANDREI *looks towards* NATASHA *and is immediately struck by her sweet, dejected face. He crosses the room towards her. The other couples stop dancing and seem to mark time.*

NATASHA *can hardly breathe as she sees him approach.*

ANDREI. Excuse me, Countess Rostova. Would you do me the honour of dancing with me?

NATASHA'*s personal music rises to a crescendo. She jumps into his arms like a ballerina. He lifts her and turns her, then puts her down again. We return to reality.*

NATASHA. Yes. Thank you.

They dance. Other couples join them. When the music stops, they look at each other, amazed at the feelings they have awakened. The COUNT *approaches.*

COUNT. Prince Andrei, how splendid to see you. You are quite recovered now, I hope.

ANDREI. Thank you. I am as well as can be expected.

COUNT. Thank God for this peace. Let's hope it lasts. So, Natasha, are you enjoying your first ball?

NATASHA. It's the loveliest time I've ever had in my life.

The focus switches to PIERRE *whose gloom is intense as he watches his wife flirting with* BORIS DRUBETSKOY *and sees them leave the room together.*

NATASHA (*coming to him*). How delightful it all is, Count. Don't you think?

PIERRE. Yes, I'm very glad. (*Suddenly.*) Natasha, do you remember when you showed me how to dance? All those years ago.

NATAHSA Of course I do. It was very funny.

PIERRE. Yes. Very funny.

Scene 7

The drawing room. The ROSTOV *house. St. Petersburg.*

NATASHA *is singing – beautifully and with no sign of giggles. The family,* PIERRE *and* ANDREI *listen in awe.*

She finishes and everyone claps. She goes to ANDREI.

NATASHA. Well, Prince Andrei, how do you like my voice?

ANDREI (*close to tears*). I like it very much. Just as I like everything you do.

NATASHA. I'm sorry . . . I mean, I wasn't asking for compliments. Oh dear . . .

ANDREI. I know you weren't.

NATASHA. You're not sad, are you?

ANDREI. No. It was only . . . your singing was so beautiful. It made me feel very close to everything that is wonderful and great inside us. And then I thought of the pettiness of our daily lives and . . . forgive me. It is foolish.

NATASHA. No, I understand. At least I think I do.

PIERRE *is watching them, as are the* COUNT *and* COUNTESS.

COUNTESS. They are falling in love, aren't they?

COUNT. How splendid. He's an excellent fellow.

COUNTESS. Yes. But I can't help feeling there is something wrong about it.

COUNT. Nonsense, little Countess. It will be one of the best matches in Russia.

Scene 8

St. Petersburg. PIERRE *is in his study with* ANDREI. NATASHA *and* SONYA *are in their bedroom.*

PIERRE. I don't know, Andrei. I haven't lost faith in the brotherhood as a whole, but the lodge here is . . . well I just don't see eye to eye with them. And somehow the magic starts to wane when you meet your fellow masons at the club or the opera and it's just plain old Count x or Prince y and they're behaving abominably. And I'm the only one who gives to charity. I don't know . . . You know they've welcomed Boris Drubetskoy to their midst?

ANDREI. I'm in love. I'm in love, my friend.

PIERRE. With Natasha Rostova?

ANDREI. Who else? I would never have believed it, but this feeling is stronger than I am. I can't live without her.

NATASHA. I never, never felt like this before. I loved Boris and my singing-teacher, but this is different. But I'm afraid when he's near me. Are you afraid of Nikolai?

SONYA. No. But you've only just met Andrei.

NATASHA. He's a grown up man, Sonya! Someone my father respects and yet he's interested in me. You don't think there's anything wrong in his being a widower, do you?

ANDREI. To think that only a few weeks ago I had given up on life. I must have seemed ridiculous. I don't care what my father thinks about the match. I have such plans for the future, Pierre.

NATASHA. Oh Sonya, isn't it thrilling? You are happy for me, aren't you?

SONYA. Of course I am.

NATASHA. I'm sure Nikolai will propose to you soon and . . .

SONYA. I don't expect anything of Nikolai. I love him and I always will, but he is perfectly free.

NATASHA. Oh, what a heart you have! If nothing came of this now, I would die.

ANDREI. The whole world is split into two halves now: she is one half, and there all is hope and light; the other is where she is not, and there all is darkness and gloom.

PIERRE. I understand that part.

ANDREI. You are happy for me, Pierre?

PIERRE. Of course I am.

ANDREI. But can she ever love me? I'm too old for her, my health isn't good.

PIERRE. She loves you. I know she does. Andrei, that girl is a treasure . . . Marry, marry her and there will be no happier man on earth.

ANDREI *goes.* NAPOLEON *appears.*

NAPOLEON. Feeling sorry for yourself again?

PIERRE. No. As it happens I am trying to fight it.

NAPOLEON. Fight what?

PIERRE. The feeling I have every day when I awaken: the feeling that life is useless and pointless.

NAPOLEON. I will tell you what your trouble is, Count Bezuhov: you are reverting to type. You are typical of the leisured and decadent class from which you sprang. You have too much time to think and too many options to choose from. You are ruined – like a blown fruit.

PIERRE. That isn't true.

NAPOLEON. You are the wealthy husband of a faithless wife. You spend your days drinking at the club, you chat to your cronies, you criticize the government – mildly and good-humouredly, of course. You have become what you always claimed to despise.

PIERRE. No!

NAPOLEON. What happened to the zeal with which you returned from France? Your dream of a Russian republic? Your desire to be me? Even your masonic nonsense was better than this. At least then you fought to improve things.

PIERRE (*shouting desperately*). And I will, I will! (*Pause.*) I don't know what to do. I want to engage in life, I do, but every time I think I've found a channel for my energies, that thought comes upon me again – that it is all pointless and everything collapses.

NAPOLEON. No. That is what is pointless, that thought you describe. You must decide what you want and do everything in your power to attain it. You must take action.

PIERRE. But to do what? I've heard it said that soldiers under fire in the trenches, when they have nothing to do, try hard to find some occupation so as to bear the danger more easily. It seems to me that we are all like those soldiers, seeking refuge from . . . from the battle which is life. Some do it in ambition, some in cards, some in making laws, some in women, some in sport, some in wine . . . Anything, so as not to think about 'it'. That terrible 'it'.

Scene 9

The ROSTOV *house. St. Petersburg.*

NATASHA *is waiting in trepidation. The* COUNTESS *enters.*

COUNTESS. Go to him, Natasha. He asks for your hand. Go.

NATASHA *runs to the ballroom where* ANDREI *is waiting.*

ANDREI. I have loved you from the moment I saw you. Do I have cause to hope? Do you love me?

NATASHA. Yes! Yes! (*She sobs and laughs.*) I am so happy.

ANDREI. Did your mother explain to you that we must wait for a year?

NATASHA (*not listening.*) I'm so happy.

ANDREI. It will be hard for us, I know, but it will give you time to be sure. Our engagement shall remain a secret. If you should come to love someone else . . .

NATASHA. Why do you say that?

ANDREI. A year is a long time.

NATASHA. What do you mean, 'a year'?

ANDREI. We must wait for a . . .

NATASHA. A whole year? But why a year? Why a year?

ANDREI. My health isn't strong. I must go abroad. And my father is insisting that we wait. Natasha, you are young, you have had so little experience . . .

NATASHA. This is awful! I shall die if I have to wait a year. It's impossible. (*Seeing the alarm on his face.*) No, no, I'm sorry. I'll do anything you ask.

ANDREI (*taking her hands*). If anything happens while I'm gone, go to Pierre. I have confided in him. He may be the most absent-minded, ridiculous fellow, but he has a heart of gold. Promise me.

NATASHA. Very well. I promise. But nothing will happen.

He kisses her hand, then, thinking again, takes her in his arms and kisses her passionately. He leaves.

NATASHA. Don't go.

But he is gone. Her mother enters.

Oh Mama, how will I ever bear it? It's awful. I will be old by the time he comes back and he won't want me anymore.

COUNTESS. No. The time will pass so quickly. We'll go to the country in the summer, and you always love that; and then before you know, it will be Christmas. Don't cry my sweet, don't cry.

Act Five

Scene 1

The PRINCE's *room. Bald Hills.*

MARIA *is in her room with little* NIKOLAI. *He is sitting at a desk trying to master the French alphabet. She is standing over him, pointer in hand. He has made another mistake.*

MARIA. No! Non, non, non! C is for chien! Chien! How many times? I'm beginning to think you are an idiot! Now you say it, Nikolai . . . C is for . . . ?

Though terrified and desperate to answer, he cannot.

Right. (*She takes him by the arm and hauls him into the corner of the room.*) You will stand there until you say it. I am not going to waste my time.

Shaking she moves back to the desk and then suddenly sits down and begins to cry.

Forgive me. Oh, forgive me. I'm so sorry.

He comes to her, crying too, and pulls her tear-wet hands from her face and kisses her. She hugs him.

Her father enters. He has a letter in his hand. She wipes her tears away hastily.

PRINCE B. For you. From Switzerland.

MARIA (*thrilled*). From Andrei? (*He hands it to her. She begins to read.*)

PRINCE B. He begs you to, 'use your influence with me', to allow him to marry that girl three months before the time on which he and I agreed.

MARIA. Natasha Rostova? Andrei is engaged to Natasha Rostova?

PRINCE B. This is what you will do: you will write and tell him to wait until I am dead. It won't be long now.

MARIA. But this is impossible. Why wasn't I told . . .

PRINCE B. Marry! Let the dear boy marry! Nice connections, has she? Clever people? Rich are they? A fine step-mother she'll make for the boy! Well, let him marry and I'll marry the little Bourienne. Oh yes! Andrei must have a step-mother too. She'll make a fine Princesse Bolkonskya. But I won't have any more women in my house. Use 'your influence' to tell him that.

MARIA *runs to the chapel, where* THEODOSIA *is praying. She falls to her knees.*

MARIA. Oh Lord, did not Your Son come down and teach us that this life is but a time of probation? And yet we cling to it and think to find happiness in it. He loved Lisa, I know he did, but that wasn't enough, and now he seeks happiness in another. And Father only objects because he wants a wealthier match. Why does no-one see? Oh Lord, what I would give to leave it all behind: this place, these people . . . Theodosia?

THEODOSIA. Yes, mistress?

MARIA. Why did you begin your pilgrimage?

THEODOSIA. No special reason, mistress. It was the natural step.

MARIA (*to God and herself again*). I'll do it. I'll take up her chains, her rags, her staff. (*Taking* THEODOSIA's *chains and winding them about herself.*) I'll wander from shrine to shrine. I'll stop at a place and pray and before I have grown used to it, I'll go on, on until my legs give way and I lie down and die and find at last that eternal peace.

Little NIKOLAI *creeps in.*

NIKOLAI. Aunt Maria? Are you coming back?

MARIA (*realising she will never leave*). Yes, my love. I'm coming back.

Scene 2

The ROSTOV *estate. Otradnoe.*

A light snow is drifting in the air. In the distance there is the sound of dogs barking and men shouting. NIKOLAI, SONYA, NATASHA *and* PETYA, *all in hunting-gear, are concealed in a copse. At* NIKOLAI's *feet are two borzoi dogs, lying quietly.* NIKOLAI *is concentrating hard on the sounds.*

NIKOLAI (*to himself*). They must be onto something . . .

PETYA. When does something happen?

SONYA. Hush, Petya. Nikolai's listening.

NIKOLAI. I told you not to come.

PETYA. 'No obstacles bar a Russian's path!'

NATASHA. Why shouldn't we come? I like hunting just as much as you do. (NIKOLAI *is listening again.*) Karay! Come here, boy. What a lovely dog he is. He remembers me from last summer.

NIKOLAI. He's not a dog, he's a harrier. (*Pause.*) Oh God, I know Thou art great and it's wrong to pray about this, but please, please make the old wolf come this way and let Karay fix his teeth in her throat and finish her off. Just once in my life, to kill an old wolf . . . that's all I want . . . that's all I want . . .

Suddenly the wolf enters, running easily, unaware of danger.

NIKOLAI. No! Oh God, it can't be.

The wolf pauses. NATASHA nudges PETYA, who stares, wide-eyed. NIKOLAI whispers.

Tally-ho!

The dogs jump up. The wolf sees NIKOLAI. Their eyes lock.

They are still for a moment and then NIKOLAI yells.

Tally-ho!

He lets the dogs go. The wolf flees. He cries out again and everyone joins in.

NIKOLAI. She's getting away. Karay, stop her!

They set off across the stage, screaming and hollering. At the other side the wolf runs on, surrounded by dogs now. Karay lunges for her throat. NIKOLAI flings himself onto the wolf, putting his foot on her throat. Other huntsmen arrive on the scene, including the ATTENDANT. NIKOLAI takes his knife from his belt.

ATTENDANT. Don't. We'll string her up.

They thrust a stake between her jaws and bind her legs. As she is brought under control, everyone cheers.

Well done, sir.

NIKOLAI (*ecstatically*). An old wolf! An old wolf!

ATTENDANT. We got four of the cubs as well – up at the Otradnoe Copse.

The wolf is surrounded. One or two of the men prod her. She jerks but is not frantic. The COUNT enters.

COUNT. What a formidable brute. An old one, eh?

ATTENDANT. That she be.

COUNT. First rate, Nikolai.

NIKOLAI. Touch her, Petya.

PETYA (*goes to*). I daren't. (*The crowd laugh.*)

SONYA. I will.

She does so. Everyone cheers. NIKOLAI *looks at her in admiration.* NATASHA *suddenly lets out a resounding, extraordinary shriek, that shatters the air.*

As everyone begins to move off, NIKOLAI *holds* SONYA *back.*

He puts his hands inside the fur hood of her cloak and pulls her to him. He kisses her, passionately.

NIKOLAI. Sonya!

Scene 3

Outside the house. Otradnoe.

It is growing dark. NATASHA *and* NIKOLAI *stand together watching the snow. Behind them, the house is lit up and the sound of the peasants singing drifts on the air.*

NATASHA. What were you thinking about just now?

NIKOLAI. Just now? I was thinking what a fine harrier Karay is and how she could out-run all the other dogs. She could, you know. (*Pause.*) What were you thinking about?

NATASHA. I was thinking that we could be anywhere. Not on the estate at all. It's like fairyland. And then I thought . . . no, that was all.

NIKOLAI. You thought about him, didn't you?

NATASHA. I know how much he would have enjoyed today.

NIKOLAI. Would he?

NATASHA. Oh yes. I know he seems serious and stern but he would have understood about the hunt and how wonderful it is to ride through the snow and how beautiful the forests are. And the dancing – he would love to watch the peasants dance. I wish he would come back.

NIKOLAI. He will. (*Pause.*) Natasha, I've made up my mind about Sonya.

NATASHA (*looking at him in astonishment and joy.*) Oh, I'm so glad. So glad. Have you told her? (*He nods. They hug, then look back at the snow.*) Nikolai?

NIKOLAI. Yes?

NATASHA. I'm sure I will never again be as happy and at peace as I am this moment.

NIKOLAI. Don't say that . . .

NATASHA. It's true. I know it's true.

*He puts his arm around her. Distant sounds of war are heard.
A threat of danger builds until the end of the act.*

Scene 4

The dining room, Bald Hills and drawing room, Otradnoe.

*At Bald Hills, MARIA, MLLE BOURIENNE and PRINCE
BOLKONSKY sit at dinner. The ATTENDANT is about to pour
wine and goes to MARIA.*

PRINCE B. Stop. From now on, I wish Mlle Bourienne to be
served first.

*The ATTENDANT obeys instructions, going to MARIA
second. There is an awkward silence. He brings something else
and, out of habit, goes to MARIA first.*

PRINCE B. How dare you? (*He flings his cane at him.*) How dare
you disobey me? I'll have you flogged! I'll have you sent to the
army. (*Pointing to MLLE BOURIENNE.*) She is the first
person in this house. She is my special friend. Get out!

*At Otradnoe, NIKOLAI is with his mother. NATASHA is
listening outside the door.*

NIKOLAI. So I intend to leave the army as soon as possible and
marry her. You know I have always loved her . . .

COUNTESS. What has love to do with it? She is penniless. She is
nobody. Does the ruin of your family mean nothing to you?

NIKOLAI. Of course, but . . .

COUNTESS. Well do it. Marry her! Andrei is marrying without
his father's blessing, why shouldn't you? But do not ever, ever,
expect me to receive that scheming creature as my daughter.

NIKOLAI. Don't start blaming Sonya.

COUNTESS. She has been angling for you from the start.

NIKOLAI. If I hear even a whisper of her being ill-used, I will
marry her without your knowledge.

COUNTESS. How dare you?

NIKOLAI. I always knew you were against us, but I never
believed you would actually try to force me to sell my feelings.
Well, this is the last time I will ever consider you in anything.
This is the last time I will . . .

NATASHA (*running in*). Nikolai, stop it! Stop it!

The COUNT enters, aghast. The COUNTESS bursts into tears.

At Bald Hills, PRINCE BOLKONSKY walks over to MLLE B.

PRINCE B. Ma chère Mademoiselle.

He fondles and kisses her. She plays up to him. He leaves.

MARIA (*suddenly*). It is loathsome, vile, inhuman to take advantage of his weakness. How could you?

She rushes to the chapel and physically punishes herself for her anger.

At Otradnoe.

COUNT (*taking* NIKOLAI *aside*). My son, you don't know how our finances have suffered of late. We have lived beyond our means . . . and then there have been extra expenses . . .

NIKOLAI. I have told you I will pay you back every penny I lost at cards . . .

COUNT. I know you will, I'm not . . . it's my fault, all my fault. We may have to sell a town-house . . .

NIKOLAI (*walking out*). If that's what it takes, then so be it.

At Bald Hills, the PRINCE *storms into the chapel.*

PRINCE B. How dare you forget yourself in her presence? I am master in this house. We must part, madam. Find a home somewhere else. And don't imagine I said that in the heat of the moment. We must part. If only some fool would take her to wife!

Scene 5

The BOLKONSKY *house. Moscow.*

The PRINCE *has a gathering of friends and sycophants about him, including* PIERRE, BORIS, PRINCE VASILI, *and* MLLE BOURIENNE *who sits beside him.* MARIA *is trying to join in, but cannot withstand her father's studied coldness.*

ALL (*raising glasses to* PRINCE). Good health!

They drink and sit. MARIA *goes and sits in a corner, unhappy and dejected.*

VASILI. You must honour us with your presence in town more often, cher Prince.

PRINCE B. I shall. Now you've all come to your senses over Bonaparte. Why would I have come to Moscow to hear of the honours heaped upon him? Well now we'll teach him a thing or two. War! War is imminent!

VASILI. One only marvels at the long-suffering or the blindness of the sovereigns. Now Bonaparte means to depose the Pope and no-one says a word. Our Emperor is the only one to raise a voice against the seizure of the Duke of Oldenburg's territory.

PRINCE B. He shifts the Dukes about as I might move my serfs from Bald Hills to my Ryazan estates. (*All laugh.*)

BORIS. The Duke of Oldenburg bears his misfortune admirably. I had the honour of being presented to him on my journey from Petersburg.

PRINCE B. Who are you? Do I know you?

BORIS. Drubetskoy, sir. Boris Drubetskoy.

VASILI. But how can we possibly make war against the French? (*Pause.*) Are not the French our Gods? Is not Paris the Kingdom of Heaven?

All laugh. PIERRE *goes to* MARIA.

PIERRE. May I sit with you a while? (*She nods.*) Have you known that young man long? Drubetskoy? I've noticed he's always to be found where there are wealthy heiresses. Would you marry him?

MARIA. Oh heavens, Count, there are moments when I would marry anybody! How bitter it is to love someone near to you and to feel . . . to feel that you can do nothing but be a trial to him. Then there is only one thing left – to go away, but where would I go? (*She cries.*)

PIERRE. Princess, what's wrong? But this is terrible. You are unhappy.

MARIA. No, no . . . please. Please. (*She wipes her eyes surreptitiously, glancing at her father.*) I hear the Rostovs will arrive in Moscow soon. What kind of girl is she, Pierre? Andrei is risking so much.

PIERRE. I'm not sure how to describe her. She's fascinating.

Scene 6

The drawing room. The BOLKONSKY *house. Moscow.*

MARIA *and* MLLE BOURIENNE *step forward to meet* NATASHA. MARIA DMITRIEVNA *looks on.* NATASHA *is dressed particularly fashionably.* MARIA *looks at her disdainfully. They sit at opposite ends of the room. Silence.*

MARIA D. The girls and their father are staying with me. There's no point heating their house for such a short visit.

MLLE BOURIENNE. But of course. And your maman is not with you?

MARIA D. The Countess has remained in the country. To rest.
Well, I shall leave you two to get better acquainted. I said
I would call on Anna Semeonovna while I am in the district.
I shall return in fifteen minutes, Natasha.

She leaves. NATASHA *and* MARIA *look alarmed.* MLLE B.
Does not realise she is 'de trop'.

MLLE BOURIENNE. It is so wonderful, is it not, to be in
Moscow. We lead rather a dull life in the country. Lise used to
say that Bald Hills was the end of the earth.

The door is flung open and PRINCE BOLKONSKY *enters
wearing a night-cap and dressing gown.* NATASHA *blushes
and curtsies.*

PRINCE B. Ah, madam, Madam Countess, Countess Rostova if
I am not mistaken. I beg your pardon, pray excuse me madam,
God is my witness, I did not know you were honouring us with
a visit. I came to see my daughter. I beg you to excuse me, I did
not know.

He looks NATASHA *over from head to foot then wanders off.*

MLLE BOURIENNE. He has not been himself of late.

MARIA. Mademoiselle, please go and see what it was my father
wanted.

NATASHA (*rising*). Please don't go on my account. I'm leaving
now.

MARIA. Wait, I must . . . (NATASHA *gives her a scornful look.*)
Natasha . . . Natalie, I want you to know how glad I am that my
brother has found happiness.

NATASHA. I think, Princess, the moment has passed for speaking
of that.

She leaves and runs to the mirror.

What have you done? How could you have said those things?
But I'm glad I said them. What right have they got to look
down on me? To insult me? I am Natasha Rostova . . . (*She
covers her eyes with her hands and tries with all her heart to
see* ANDREI. *He enters and goes to her and embraces her.*)
Andrei . . . where are you? Please, please come back.

Scene 7

The Opera House. Moscow.

NATASHA, SONYA, COUNT ROSTOV and MARIA DIMITRI-
EVNA *sit in one box.* HÉLÈNE *and her entourage sit in the
adjoining one.*

The overture has just begun. SONYA *whispers to* NATASHA.

SONYA. Look, there's Boris with his new fiancée.

NATASHA. I'm pleased for him. He couldn't have made a more successful match.

The COUNT *leans over to* HÉLÈNE.

COUNT. Have you been in Moscow long, Countess? I'll call and kiss your hand, if I may. Is Pierre here?

HÉLÈNE. He's in Kiev. I'm sure he'll call when he returns.

COUNT (*whispering to* NATASHA). Wonderful, isn't she?

NATASHA. Yes. I can see why people fall in love with her.

ANATOLE *and* DOLOHOV *enter and, swaggering through the stalls, take their seats on the front row.*

COUNT. There's her brother. How alike they are. He and Dolohov have broken every heart in Moscow. The rascals!

ANATOLE *turns and smiles at his sister. He notices* NATASHA *and stares at her for far too long.* NATASHA *blushes.*

ANATOLE *nudges* DOLOHOV *and points her out. They whisper. He looks back at her. The opera begins and demands attention but after a moment or two,* ANATOLE *gets up and walks towards her box. Once underneath, to her absolute horror, he begins to sing.*

No-one else sees or hears, though she feels everyone must be able to.

ANATOLE (*sung*). Who is this charming, tender creature? So real and yet so distant. How delicate her arm, how white her skin, her neck, her bosom . . . I do believe I've lost my heart, I do believe I've lost my heart.

The opera music now seems to fit around his phrases. He bounds up to his sister's box and whispers to her.

HÉLÈNE. Count, you must introduce me to your daughters. The whole town is singing their praises.

COUNT. Natasha, Sonya, this is Countess Bezuhov. (*The girls curtsey.*)

HÉLÈNE. Please let Natasha come and sit with me. We must become better acquainted. (NATASHA *goes and sits next to* HÉLÈNE.) Oh! And this is my brother, Anatole.

They watch the opera.

ANATOLE (*sung*). I fear you won't believe me, but I have seen you once before. There was a ball on New Year's Eve . . . do you recall? The charms of this great city had been lost on me thus far, but now I find that I'm in heaven and you are the only star. Hélène is holding a recital, please tell me you will come . . .

ALL (HÉLÈNE *and her box,* DOLOHOV *and men. Sung*). Please tell him you will come.

NATASHA (*sung*). I will come.

ALL (*sung*). She will come.

ANATOLE (*sung*). I do believe I've lost my heart, I do believe I've lost my heart.

All stand and clap and then leave the boxes. NATASHA *goes to* SONYA *and clings to her arm.*

NATASHA. Sonya, you know that man?

SONYA. Anatole Kuragin?

NATASHA. Yes. Did you notice anything strange in his behaviour?

SONYA. No. He's terribly handsome, isn't he?

The guests at HÉLÈNE'*s recital take their seats.* NATASHA *and* SONYA *enter with* COUNT ROSTOV. HÉLÈNE *greets them.*

HÉLÈNE. I'm so pleased, so pleased that you have come. (*To* NATASHA.) Even if you are engaged, I cannot think your fiancé would wish you to shut yourself up like a nun. (*Drawing her to one side.*) I dined with my brother yesterday, and we nearly died of laughter. He eats nothing and can only sigh. He is madly in love with you, my charmer.

NATASHA *blushes – but with excitement now. She takes her place beside everyone else.* ANATOLE *appears behind her.*

ANATOLE (*sung*). From the moment I first saw you, I have loved you and adored you.

NATASHA. Do not say such things to me.

ANATOLE (*sung*). You've bewitched me, can't you see?

NATASHA (*running to a corner*). I am betrothed, I love another.

ANATOLE (*sung*). What has that to do with me? (*Speaking.*) I cannot come to call on you, but is it possible I am never to see you? I love you to distraction. We two were meant to be. (*Sung.*) Natalie?

He can tell she is weakening. HÉLÈNE *approaches.*

(*Speaking.*) Take this note. Read it. Send word to me and I will come for you. One word, Natalie. (*Sung.*) I do believe I've lost my heart.

HÉLÈNE (*sung*). I do believe he's lost his heart.

NATASHA (*sung*). I do believe I've lost my heart.

ALL (*sung*). I do believe they've/we've lost our hearts, lost our hearts, lost our hearts.

Scene 8

NATASHA's *room.* MARIA DMITRIEVNA's *house. Moscow.*

NATASHA *is standing infront of the mirror. She looks at herself in a new light – as a sexual being.*

SONYA *enters. She picks up a note from beside the bed and reads it. She looks at* NATASHA *in astonishment and pain.*

NATASHA (*without looking round*). I'm glad you've read it. I wanted you to know.

SONYA. It can't be true. What about Andrei? How can you have loved one man for a whole year and suddenly . . . you have only met him twice!

NATASHA. Sonya darling, I have heard of this happening. The moment I saw him I felt he was my master and I his slave. Whatever he tells me to do, I shall do it.

SONYA. For God's sake, Natasha, how could you have let things go so far?

NATASHA. Don't you understand? I have no will anymore. I love him and that's all I know.

SONYA. What if he is not an honourable man?

NATASHA. Not honourable? How can you doubt him?

SONYA. If he's honourable, why doesn't he come to the house? He should declare his intentions or give you up. And if you won't tell him that, I will. And I'll tell Papa.

NATASHA. Don't you dare. Don't dare even think of telling anyone. Soon it will all be over and I will be gone from here and I won't trouble your conscience anymore.

SONYA. You are going away with him, aren't you? Oh my God, you are eloping.

NATASHA. Leave me alone.

SONYA. Natasha . . . Natasha, think what you are doing. Please. You are rushing to your ruin.

NATASHA (*cold and spiteful*). Then I'll go to my ruin and the sooner the better. And if you tell anyone about this I will hate you for the rest of your life.

SONYA. Natasha . . .

NATASHA. I hate you already.

Scene 9

MARIA DMITRIEVNA's *house, Moscow.*

NATASHA *is waiting in her room. She has a cloak on.*

In the courtyard, ANATOLE *and* DOLOHOV *enter.* ANATOLE *is wearing a fur cloak and carrying another.*

ANATOLE. Wait here.

He approaches the house. The ATTENDANT *appears and blocks his retreat.*

ATTENDANT. Kindly walk this way to the mistress.

ANATOLE. What mistress? Who are you?

In NATASHA's *bedroom.* MARIA DMITRIEVNA *marches in.* SONYA *hovers in the doorway.*

MARIA D. You shameless hussy!

She pushes the astonished NATASHA *back onto the bed.*

ATTENDANT. Kindly step in. My mistress's orders are to bring you inside.

Another servant is attempting to apprehend DOLOHOV.

DOLOHOV. Kuragin! Come back! Treachery!

A struggle commences.

In the bedroom, NATASHA *hides her face in the bed.*

MARIA D. Disgusting, abominable behaviour in my house. You shameless wench. It's no use lying to me. (*Shaking her by the arm.*) Listen when I speak to you.

ANATOLE *and* DOLOHOV *manage to free themselves and run off.*

You have disgraced yourself like a common hussy. I can't tell you what I would do to you if I had my way.

NATASHA's *body begins to heave with sobs. The* ATTENDANT *enters and whispers to* MARIA D. *He leaves.*

He's escaped – luckily for him. But I'll catch up with him. Do you hear me? (*She turns* NATASHA *towards her and is shocked by her expression.* NATASHA *wrenches herself free and turns back to the bed.*) Natalie, I wish for your good. Stay like that, I won't touch you. But do you realise how wrongly you've acted? If your father or brother were to hear of this, they would challenge him – is that what you want? What about your betrothed?

NATASHA. I have no betrothed. I have written. I have broken it off.

MARIA D. Kuragin is a scoundrel, a knave . . .

NATASHA. He's better than any of you! Sonya, how could you have done this to me? Go away! You all hate me!

MARIA D. Sonya, tell the servants to bring some lime-flower water. And two extra quilts.

SONYA *goes.* MARIA D. *sits down next to* NATASHA *and strokes her hair.*

Scene 10

PIERRE'*s house. Moscow.*

ANATOLE *and* HÉLÈNE *are talking.* PIERRE *walks in.*

HÉLÈNE. Ah, Pierre. You don't know what a plight our poor Anatole is in.

PIERRE (*stopping abruptly infront of her*). Wherever you are, depravity and evil are to be found. (*He goes to* ANATOLE *and takes him by the arm.*) Come with me.

HÉLÈNE. If you dare, in my drawing room to . . .

PIERRE *drags* ANATOLE *into the study and grabs him by the collar.*

PIERRE. You are a scoundrel and a blackguard. Did you promise to marry her?

ANATOLE. I . . . I didn't . . . I never promised because . . .

PIERRE. Because you are married already. Did you think I didn't know about your sordid little affair in Poland? Where do you think the money comes from that you send to that girl each month? Natasha Rostova is seriously ill. Did you know? When she found out you were married she took poison.

ANATOLE. Who told her? What a mean trick.

PIERRE. Do you have any of her letters? Letters!

ANATOLE *takes a letter from his pocket and hands it over.*

Tomorrow you will leave Moscow.

ANATOLE. But how can I?

PIERRE. There is such a thing as other people's happiness and peace of mind. You would ruin a whole life for the sake of a little amusement. Amuse yourself with women like my wife, they are armed against you by a similar depravity. What you have done is as base as hitting an old man or a child.

ANATOLE. I don't know about that and I don't want to, but you have used words to me – talk of being base and so on – which, as a man of honour I can't allow.

PIERRE. Is it satisfaction you want?

ANATOLE. At least you can retract what you've said. If you want me to do as you wish, that is.

PIERRE (*disgusted*). I will then. I take it back. I beg you to forgive me. And if you require money for your journey . . . (ANATOLE *smiles, a base cringing smile.*) Oh, you vile, heartless breed!

He leaves.

Scene 11

The study. The BOLKONSKY house. Moscow.

ANDREI *is collecting NATASHA's letters together. PIERRE is sitting awkwardly, unsure of what to say.*

PIERRE. You look well. Was the treatment a success?

ANDREI. Oh yes. I'm jolly well now. I have received my dismissal from Countess Rostova. Here are her letters and her portrait. Kindly return them to her – if you happen to be passing.

PIERRE. She is very ill. She took poison.

ANDREI. I'm sorry to hear that. So, I take it Monsieur Kuragin has not honoured her with his hand.

PIERRE. He could not have married her. He is married already.

ANDREI (*laughing like his father*). And where is your brother-in-law now, if I may ask?

PIERRE. He's gone to . . . I don't really know.

ANDREI. Well. No matter. Tell Countess Rostova from me that she was and is perfectly free and I wish her all happiness. (*He hands the letters to* PIERRE.)

PIERRE. What are your plans now?

ANDREI. I'm returning to the army. We will soon be at war.

PIERRE. I thought you had done with all that.

ANDREI. This is different. I don't want to see Napoleon in Moscow.

PIERRE. Yes. I'm considering raising a regiment. What do you think?

ANDREI. Why not?

PIERRE. Andrei, is there any chance that you might forgive her? She is so young and . . .

ANDREI. I'm sorry, but I'm not equal to following where that gentleman has trodden. If you wish to remain my friend, never speak to me of this again.

Scene 12

MARIA. DMITRIEVNA's *house. Moscow.*

NATASHA. *stands in front of the mirror. She looks thin and broken. She tries to sing.*

NATASHA. Isn't . . . that . . .

She keeps opening her mouth but no sound will come out.
She suddenly hurls her arms at the glass and tries to smash it.

PIERRE *enters. He pauses for a moment, shocked by her appearance.*

NATASHA. Thank you for agreeing to see me. Prince Bolkonsky . . . he once told me to turn to you. Tell him to forgive me. Oh, I know all is over between us, I have no illusions, but please beg him to forgive me for everything. (*She sinks to her knees, trembling.*)

PIERRE. I will, of course I will. But Natasha, I must ask you one thing – did you really love that horrible man?

NATASHA. He's not horrible! Oh, I don't know, I don't know anything. (*She begins to cry.*)

PIERRE. (*overwhelmed with pity*). Yes, of course. Of course. We won't speak of it. You know, I should be very happy if you would look on me as your friend. If you need help or simply to open your heart to someone, think of me.

NATASHA. Don't speak to me like that. I'm not worthy of it.

She tries to run away but he catches hold of her hand.

PIERRE. You have your whole life before you.

NATASHA. No. It's all over.

PIERRE. All over? If I were not myself, but the handsomest, cleverest, best man in the world, and if I were free, I would be on my knees this minute to beg for your hand and your love.

NATASHA *looks into his eyes for a moment, weeping tears of gratitude. Then she runs off.* PIERRE *wipes the tears from his own eyes and smiles. Outside, he throws open his coat and fills his lungs with the frosty air. He looks up at the sky.* NAPOLEON *appears and watches.*

I feel for her, I feel so much for that . . . girl, that little piece of humanity. Oh, what a life! How can I have been so blind? How can anything be pointless while she is in the world, while my spirits can soar so high? I love her. I love her, and no-one will ever know.

ATTENDANT. Where to now, your excellency?

All around PIERRE, *the injured of the play have gathered –* MARIA, ANDREI, PRINCE BOLKONSKY, NIKOLAI, *the* COUNTESS *– everyone in fact. They walk forward and then collapse down as though they have been shot, then pull themselves up and walk forward again.*

Act Six

Scene 1

Borodino. The eve of battle. In the Russian camp, the troops are organizing themselves. There are carts and tents and camp-fires scattered about and smoke fills the air.

PIERRE enters and stands at the top of a hill. He surveys the scene, beside himself with excitement. He is dressed in a green swallow-tail coat and a tall white hat and this, coupled with his lack of occupation, makes him stand out like a sore thumb. Two OFFICERS rush to and fro.

PIERRE. Excuse me, would you have the goodness to tell me the name of the village opposite?

OFFICER. Burdino, isn't it?

OFFICER. Borodino. (*He goes on his way.*)

PIERRE. Is this where the battle will be tomorrow?

OFFICER. Here or here abouts.

PIERRE. Excellent. Could you explain some things to me? I can't quite make sense of it. I suppose I was expecting a big field. Are those our men?

OFFICER. Yes. And the French are over there.

PIERRE. Where? Where?

OFFICER. You can just see them. There.

PIERRE. Oh yes! So those are the French. Incredible. Is Napoleon there, then?

At this point, NAPOLEON and his entourage enter and set up camp.

OFFICER. I should think so. He stays close to the front.

PIERRE. Wonderful. So how will it all work? Where's our position?

He pursues the OFFICERS across the stage.

NAPOLEON *is behind a screen in his tent, being dressed by two VALETS. One is combing his hair whilst another sprays him with cologne. He is impatient. The muscles in his left calf twitch continuously. His* AIDE-DE-CAMP *stands nearby, awaiting orders.*

NAPOLEON (*to* AIDE) Take this down. Soldiers! The battle you have longed for is at hand. Victory depends on you. It is essential for us: it will give us comfortable quarters and a speedy return to our own country. Acquit yourselves as you did at Austerlitz, Friedland, Vitebsk and Smolensk. Let posterity recall with pride your achievements this day. May it be said of each man among you, 'He was in the great battle before Moscow'. Short and to the point. Have it circulated before dawn. (*To* VALETS.) Enough, enough. Where is Monsieur de Beausset? I will receive him now.

He walks into the main part of the tent where he catches the prefect of the French palace hastily preparing a surprise for him. He pretends not to notice and tugs the courtier's ear in a patronising way.

I am sorry to have given you such a long journey, De Beausset.

BEAUSSET. Sire, I expected nothing less than to find you at the gates of Moscow.

NAPOLEON *smiles smugly and then pretends to notice the surprise for the first time.*

NAPOLEON. Ah! But what have we here?

BEAUSSET (*unveiling a portrait*). A present to Your Majesty from the Empress.

NAPOLEON. The King of Rome. My little son. Admirable.

He clicks his fingers and the AIDE *places a chair beneath him. He sits and gazes at the portrait, seemingly overcome.*

On the hill, a DOCTOR *approaches* PIERRE.

DOCTOR. Count! Your Excellency, I thought it was you. What brings you here?

PIERRE. Hello, Doctor. I wanted to have a look, see for myself where history is being made. Actually what I really want is to take part. I want to be able to say, 'I fought in the battle for Moscow'.

DOCTOR. You should apply directly to Kutuzov. Don't wander about God knows where, you'll miss things.

PIERRE. Is the Commander-in-chief here?

DOCTOR. Yes. That way, on the road towards Gorky.

KUTUZOV *and his entourage enter and set up camp.*

I'd take you there myself but I'm up to here. You know, Count, out of an army of a hundred thousand men, we must expect at least twenty thousand casualties tomorrow, and we haven't stretchers or surgeons enough for six. We shall just have to do our best, I suppose. (*He goes on his way.*)

PIERRE. Yes, Doctor, do your best. Good luck.

NAPOLEON (*standing suddenly.*) Take him to the front of the tent. The Old Guard must not be deprived of seeing my son and heir. It will cheer their hearts.

The AIDE *leaves with the portrait.*

So, De Beausset, what are they saying in Paris?

BEAUSSET. Sire, all Paris regrets your absence.

NAPOLEON. And what news from Spain?

BEAUSSET (*uncomfortably*). I have no definite word . . .

NAPOLEON. What news?

BEAUSSET. Sire, your army is fighting before Salamanca with heroism and devotion . . . I fear however that the outcome of the battle may not be . . .

NAPOLEON. Yes, yes. Of course. I did not expect matters to go otherwise without me there to direct them. (*He is angry and paces the room.*) Well, I must make up for it tomorrow. What a fool Alexander has been! What could he wish for that he would not have secured through my friendship? He might have extended Russia from the Gulf of Bothnia to the mouth of the Danube. Catherine the Great could not have done more. But no! He has preferred to surround himself with my enemies. What a glorious reign, what a glorious reign the Emperor Alexander's might have been! Tomorrow we shall have Kutuzov to deal with. Do you know, at Braunau he was in command of an army for three weeks and never once mounted a horse to inspect his entrenchments? We shall see.

KUTUZOV *is sitting on a bench outside his tent. There is a book in his lap. His eyes are closed and he appears to be asleep. His* AIDE *stands close by waiting for him to sign the last of several papers. He is unsure what to do.* ANDREI *stands in the background, watching.*

AIDE. There is one more paper for Your Highness to sign. (*No response.*) General Kutuzov, Sir?

KUTUZOV (*with his eyes closed*). Concerning what?

AIDE. Recovery of compensation, upon application by landowners, for the loss of oats. When the men take the crops, it is, technically, looting and . . .

KUTUZOV. Burn it. I tell you once and for all, my dear fellow, let 'em cut the crops and chop wood to their hearts' content. I don't give permission but I won't pursue the matter either. One must take life as it comes. Leave me now. I want to finish my chapter.

The AIDE *leaves.* ANDREI *is about to go too.*

KUTUZOV. Not you, Bolkonsky. I forgot you were here. Sit down, sit down. (ANDREI *does so.*) Well, young man, I have sent for you to keep you with me.

ANDREI. I thank Your Highness, but I'm afraid I'm no longer suitable for staff work. I've grown used to my regiment. I'm fond of the men and I like to think they're fond of me, too.

KUTUZOV. Pity. You would have been useful to me. But you're right. Advisers are plentiful but men are scarce. I remember you at Austerlitz . . . yes, I remember you with the standard. (ANDREI *smiles gratefully.*) Advisers, advisers. There are always those keen to give advice. Tomorrow I shall be surrounded by them; some will say, 'Do this', some will say, 'Do that'. So what am I to do? I tell you what I will do, young man – I will do nothing. Dans le doubt, abstiens-toi. Patience and time are the two most powerful warriors. Patience and time.

On the hill, DOLOHOV *approaches* PIERRE.

DOLOHOV. Count Bezuhov, I'm very glad to meet you here.

PIERRE. Dolohov . . .

DOLOHOV. On the eve of a day which God alone knows who of us is fated to survive, I am glad to have the opportunity of telling you how sorry I am for the misunderstandings which have existed between us, and I should like you to have no ill-feelings towards me. I beg you to forgive me.

PIERRE (*overcome*). Yes, yes . . . my dear fellow, I forgive you. And you forgive me, please.

DOLOHOV *embraces and kisses* PIERRE *with tears in his eyes. He goes on his way.*

Good luck, Dolohov. How right he is! This is a momentous time. How noble. How good.

In his tent, NAPOLEON *is dictating to his* AIDE. DE BEAUSSET *listens.*

NAPOLEON. Finally, the Viceroy will occupy the village, march on the redoubt and come into line with the rest of the army. All these directions must be carried out in good order, taking care to keep troops in reserve.

BEAUSSET. Excellent dispositions, Your Highness.

NAPOLEON. Do you know, De Beausset, what military art is? But of course you don't, you are a courtier, not a general. It is the art of being stronger than the enemy at a given moment. Voilà tout. The chess-board is set, tomorrow we begin the game.

ANDREI *is about to leave* KUTUZOV *alone.*

KUTUZOV. How is your father?

ANDREI. Not in strong health. I think the war is affecting him more than he admits.

KUTUZOV. Yes. He is a true Russian.

ANDREI. Confidentially, sir, if the French were to break through tomorrow, they would be passing Bald Hills within two days. My family will have left but the estate would fall into Bonaparte's hands. I don't know if my father could bear it.

Pause. KUTUZOV *has taken all this in and sees the wider implications. Tears well in his eyes. He wipes them away, unashamedly.*

KUTUZOV. Oh dear . . . what a pass they have brought us to. But give me time, young man. I won't scheme or start anything tomorrow, events will take their course, but I tell you one thing – we shall win. We shall win because we are Russians and because this is our soil and our spirit will never surrender. We shall make them eat horse-flesh yet.

ANDREI *leaves. He pauses, thinking of his family.*

At Bald Hills, MARIA *enters her father's room. He is writing. He looks up, but then leaves her waiting for a moment.*

PRINCE B. What took you so long? Come here, come here. (*She approaches*.) Well madam, the time is upon us. You and the boy must leave for Moscow. I myself shall remain here and defend Bald Hills. I shall be captured or killed. Go tonight. I don't want you here in the morning.

MARIA. No. No, Father. Nikolai may go. Everyone may go but I will not leave Bald Hills until you do.

PRINCE B. What's this? You will leave tonight, madam. That is final.

MARIA. No, Father, I will not.

PRINCE B. 'No, Father, I will not'? 'No, Father, I will not'? Who are you to say no to me? Who are you? Eh? 'No, Father, I will not'! I'll tell you who you are. You are the bane of my existence. Yes! You have worn me down to nothing with your God and your damned judgemental eyes! 'No, Father, I will not'? I know what you think of me, I know what evil thoughts you harbour in your soul. A dotard, am I? A fool? You have turned my son against me, you have molly-coddled the backbone out of the boy, you have made it your object to poison my existence. Get out of here. You will leave tonight.

MARIA. No, Father . . .

PRINCE B. I will have you torn from here by force!

MARIA *says nothing. He falls silent. He has shocked himself. He begins to tremble.*

Well, do what you want. Stay or go, but just be sure, just be sure, madam, that I never set eyes on you again.

The trembling increases. It racks his body. He collapses.

MARIA. Father! Father! Help me! Help me!

PIERRE *runs down the hill to* ANDREI.

PIERRE. Andrei! Andrei!

ANDREI *comes out of his reverie and looks at him.*

ANDREI. Good God. What are you doing here?

They embrace. ANDREI *is not pleased to see his friend.*

PIERRE. I just had to come. It's incredibly interesting. It's not at all how I'd imagined. Is it always like this?

ANDREI *begins walking quickly through the crowds of soldiers towards his quarters.* PIERRE *runs to keep up.*

PIERRE. I'm so impressed! All these men, getting on with their jobs, knowing they might die tomorrow and yet not one of them speaks of fear.

ANDREI. I thought Freemasons were against war. I'm sure you're not supposed to find it 'incredibly interesting'. (*He enters his quarters.* PIERRE *falls over something in the doorway and swears.*) Make yourself comfortable.

PIERRE. Actually. I've decided I want to take part in the battle. I want to do something useful. (*No response.*) I've had a good look at the battlefield. An officer explained it all to me.

ANDREI. So you understand the disposition of our troops?

PIERRE. Yes. Well, I understand the general layout.

ANDREI. You understand more than anyone else, then.

PIERRE. Surely you must all have an idea of the plan of action?

ANDREI. No-one does. Not even the Commander-in-chief knows how things will proceed.

PIERRE. I thought you liked Kutuzov. I thought he was an able general.

ANDREI. And what is an 'able general'?

PIERRE. Someone who gets it right. Someone who foresees the adversary's intentions.

ANDREI. No-one can do that. Kutuzov is an able general precisely because he understands that events cannot be controlled. To my mind, tomorrow means this . . .

He looks up to see CAPTAIN TIMOHIN *in the doorway.*

Come in, Captain. To my mind, a hundred thousand Russians and a hundred thousand French will meet to fight, and the side that fights the more savagely and spares itself the least will win. That side will be ours. Am I right, Captain?

TIMOHIN Yes, sir. Who would spare himself now? The soldiers in my batallion won't touch their vodka. 'It's not a time for that', they say.

ANDREI. Timohin and I came through Austerlitz together.

TIMOHIN. Yes. I had that honour. Will there be anything else, sir? If not, I'll say my prayers and get some sleep.

ANDREI. Nothing else.

TIMOHIN. Goodnight then, sir.

He gives a little bow to PIERRE *and goes on his way.*

PIERRE. Good luck, Captain.

ANDREI. I tell you one thing I would do, if I had the power –
I would take no prisoners. The French are my enemies, they
want to control my country. They must be put to death. I don't
care what was said at Tilsit.

PIERRE. Yes. Splendid. I agree with you.

ANDREI. We play at being magnanimous – chivalry and flags of
truce, but such sensibility is like that of the lady who faints at
the sight of a calf being killed but tucks into fricassée of veal
with relish. If there were none of this magnanimity we would
only ever fight for something worth facing certain death for –
as now. War isn't a polite recreation or a good career, war is
murder. (*He stops, suddenly very disturbed.*) I have begun to
understand too much. It doesn't do for a man to taste of the tree
of knowledge of good and evil . . .

PIERRE. What is it, Andrei? Tell me.

ANDREI. Never mind. It won't be for long, anyway. You go back
to where you are staying now.

PIERRE. No. I want to stay with you.

ANDREI. No. We all need a good night's sleep before battle. Even
you. (*He embraces him quickly.*) Go now. Whether we meet
again or . . . just go.

PIERRE *leaves and stands alone for a moment.*

PIERRE. My friend. My friend . . .

*There is a sudden commotion as the church procession from
Borodino approaches. Soldiers cry out – 'They're bringing
her!', 'She's coming!'.*

(*To a passing soldier.*) What's happening?

SOLDIER They're bringing her, our Holy Mother of God, the
Holy Mother of Smolensk.

A company of infantry enter, preceding the icon. PRIESTS *can
be seen next, and* DEACONS *and* CHORISTERS. *All are
chanting. The huge icon is born in on the shoulders of several
soldiers. Men everywhere drop what they are doing and bow
down to the ground. The procession comes to a halt. A new
group of* SOLDIERS *takes the burden of the icon.*

The crowd parts, as KUTUZOV *makes his way to the front and
slowly sinks to his knees. Everyone else follows suit, including*
ANDREI, DOLOHOV, ANATOLE *and* NIKOLAI.

At Bald Hills, MARIA *kneels to pray.*

In Moscow, NATASHA *arrives in church, supported by her
mother and* SONYA *and kneels to pray.*

PRIEST. Oh Mother of God, save thy servants from all adversities.

DEACON. For to thee under God every man doth flee as to a steadfast bulwark and defence.

ANDREI. Oh Lord, it's as well that only You can look into my heart and read how black my thoughts are. How deceived I have been in this life. Everything I have clung to is an illusion. I see that now. Honour? It disintegrated in my hand even as I grasped it. Love? A naive and foolish dream. Now I go about pretending it is love for my homeland which spurs me on. But do I really care? What would it matter if we lost Bald Hills? Was it ever ours to lose? What if the French over-run half Russia? Would things be any worse than they are now?

PRIEST. In peace let us pray unto the Lord.

DEACON. As one community, without distinction of class, united in brotherly love, let us pray.

NATASHA. Oh Lord, I know I have been wicked, more wicked than anyone has ever been, but show me how to be good and I will never stray again.

PRIEST. Let us commit ourselves and our lives to Christ the Lord.

NATASHA. Commit ourselves to God. Oh God, I submit myself to thee. I ask for nothing, I desire nothing. Teach me how to act, what to do with my will. Take me, take me to thee.

MARIA. Oh Lord, I pray that my father might be made well again. I pray that in Your mercy . . . I don't. I want him to die. I want it to be over. I want his suffering to end. I want to be set free from this bondage. I want love. I want my freedom. I want my life.

PRIEST. Almighty God, strengthen our most gracious Sovereign Lord, the Emperor Alexander Pavlovich. Bless his counsels and his deeds. Put weapons of steel in the hands of those who go forth in thy name and gird their loins with strength for the battle.

ANDREI. Will I die tomorrow, Lord? Yes. I will be killed. Perhaps not even by the enemy but by one of my own side. And the French will come along and take me by head and heels and throw me into a hole so that I don't stink under their noses. And life will go on . . . just as naturally as it did before. Life will go on and I will cease to be.

PRIEST. Lord, thou art able to save great things and small. Thou art God, and man cannot prevail against thee. Amen.

As they kneel with their heads on the earth, night passes and the first light of dawn begins to fill the sky. A drum begins to beat. All rise with expressions of profound concentration and take their positions.

NAPOLEON *stands at the top of the hill and surveys the scene.*
KUTUZOV *goes to stand at the other side of the hill and does*
likewise. PIERRE *stands in between them.*

Silence. As the sun rises fully in the sky, NAPOLEON *raises*
his arm and lowers it and a moment later the first cannon-ball
explodes over Borodino.

The emphasis of the battle should be PIERRE's *changing*
attitude to it. At first it should seem extremely beautiful, like
a sound and light show, with swirling mist and violet smoke,
brilliant sunshine and gleaming dew, the flash of steel, the silk
standards, the white church glistening in the distance, the
moving bodies of soldiers in uniform.

PIERRE. How beautiful . . .

He is awe-struck by the most fantastic sight he has ever seen.

Then fighting begins in earnest. The lines of charging men
come over the hill again and again. Some fall. The gestures
of war become more extreme.

PIERRE *wants to join in, but he is ordered out of the way by*
an irate officer.

OFFICER What's that fellow doing infront of the line? Get out of
the way!

NIKOLAI, ANATOLE *and* DOLOHOV *line up to charge.*
The sounds of the battle become muted and they fall into slow
motion as we enter their thoughts.

NIKOLAI. How glorious the sky is. How brilliant the sun. There,
all is peace. I would wish for nothing, nothing in the world, if
only I could be there.

ANATOLE. Who are those men? Are they running at me? Why?
To kill me? Me, who everyone is so fond of? Me, who is so
beautiful?

DOLOHOV. I am crossing the line between life and death. I have
been there before and I am not afraid. I have been there before
and I am not afraid . . .

They wind themselves up for the charge until the tension
becomes too great and they move forward – slowly at first then
faster and wilder. The sounds of the battle crash in around
them. There is smoke and confuson. ANATOLE *falls.*

On the hill, PIERRE *is looking worried. He can't make sense of*
it any more. It seems to be out of control. He calls out to an
OFFICER *who is rushing up to* KUTUZOV.

PIERRE. What's happening? Is this supposed to be happening?

OFFICER. Your Serene Highness, Sir, I am honoured to report that General Murat has been taken prisoner.

Those around congratulate themselves.

KUTUZOV. We must not crow too soon, gentlemen. There is nothing extraordinary in the capture of a general. But I believe the battle is ours. Ride down the line and spread news of Murat.

OFFICER. Sir!

He turns and sets off down the hill. PIERRE *follows.*

PIERRE. Wait, I'm coming with you. Wait.

He catches him and clasps his arm just as the OFFICER *takes a bullet in the back. His body crumples.* PIERRE *eases him to the ground. He looks about and becomes aware of other bodies. A* SOLDIER *begins to scream continually. Horses are groaning and whining. Two men push past carrying an injured man across their muskets.* PIERRE *wants to help but they are gone. He realises he has arrived in hell.*

On the hill, an OFFICER *approaches* NAPOLEON (*who is drinking punch*).

OFFICER. Your Majesty, the King of Naples requests me to inform you that the Russians will be routed if Your Majesty will allow him one more division.

NAPOLEON. Reinforcements? So soon? Impossible. Tell the King of Naples that it is not yet noon and I do not yet see my chess-board clearly. Go.

Down the hill, PIERRE *is still stumbling about through the carnage. He has lost his hat and his coat and shirt are covered in blood.*

PIERRE. Let me help. Please let me help.

Nearby, ANDREI *is standing with* TIMOHIN.

TIMOHIN. How much longer, sir? We can't keep them standing here much longer.

ANDREI. I know. But there's nothing I can do.

TIMOHIN. I've lost a third of mine and we haven't even moved. The waste, sir . . .

Suddenly someone shouts out – 'Look out.' A shell lands a couple of yards away, spinning furiously.

(*Taking cover.*) Get down !

But ANDREI *just stands, watching it whirl and hiss. It explodes.* ANDREI *falls.* TIMOHIN *cries out and runs to him.*

TIMOHIN. Your Excellency! Prince! Prince!

On the hill, a GENERAL *approaches* NAPOLEON.

GENERAL. Sire, reinforcements. We need reinforcements!

NAPOLEON. No. I have never before released reinforcements at this stage and I shall not do so now.

DOLOHOV *approaches* KUTUZOV.

DOLOHOV. Sir, General Raevsky wishes me to report that the troops are standing their ground and the French have ceased the attack.

A GENERAL *approaches.*

GENERAL. Sir, all the points of our position are in the enemy's hands. We must retreat.

DOLOHOV. We are in an excellent position to attack.

GENERAL. The men are running away and it's impossible to stop them. I cannot conceal from Your Highness what I have seen. We must retreat.

KUTUZOV. You have seen? You have seen? (*He rises.*) How dare you, sir? The real course of the battle is better known to me, the Commander-in-Chief. I will hear no mention of retreat. Your information is wrong and I thank you not to repeat it.

At the dressing station, hundreds of soldiers are awaiting attention. TIMOHIN *arrives with* ANDREI, *who is unconcious.*

A DOCTOR *comes out. It is the same one whom* PIERRE *met the previous day. His arms are covered in blood.*

DOCTOR. Who is that?

TIMOHIN. Prince Bolkonsky.

DOCTOR. Bring him straight in.

SOLDIER. Typical. Even in heaven they're going to jump the queue.

ANDREI. *is laid down. Nearby a man is having his leg amputated. He screams in pain. The* DOCTOR *goes to help.* TIMOHIN *kisses* ANDREI *and leaves.* ANDREI *sits up a little and looks across to the screaming man.*

ANATOLE. Show me! (*He is helped to sit up.*) Show me! Oh . . . oh no, oh no.

ANDREI *stares at him. He feels that he knows him but is not sure why.* NATASHA *enters, dressed as she was at the ball. She is singing. She stops and looks up.*

NATASHA. What does it all mean, Andrei?

She disappears. ANATOLE *cries out again.* ANDREI *begins to cry, a child's tears.*

ANDREI. God help him. God help him.

At Bald Hills. MARIA *arrives at her father's bedside.* MLLE BOURIENNE *is already there.*

MLLE BOURIENNE. The Doctor has left for Moscow. He won't come back. What are we going to do, Princesse?

MARIA *takes her father's feeble hand and kisses it. He tries to speak. At first the sounds are indistinct. He tries again.*

I'm so sorry. I cannot understand. All night he has been trying to . . .

The PRINCE *is still trying to articulate.*

MARIA. My soul is troubled?

He bellows in confirmation. He takes her hand and begins clasping it frantically to different parts of his breast as if he can't find the right place for it.

PRINCE B. I called for you. Why didn't you come?

MARIA. If only I had known. I was afraid. I thought you didn't want me . . .

PRINCE B. Thank you . . . daughter dearest . . . for all . . . forgive . . . forgive . . . forgive . . . Andrei!

MARIA. He's with the army, mon père, at Borodino.

PRINCE Yes. Russia is lost. They have destroyed her. (*He begins to weep. Then, after a moment he utters something unintelligible. He repeats it.*) Put on your white dress. I like it.

MARIA *sobs. The* PRINCE *dies.* MLLE BOURIENNE *weeps.*

MARIA. No. No, oh no, oh no. Father, I love you.

KUTUZOV *is sitting on the bench. His* AIDE *stands beside him.*

AIDE. All the generals are here now, sir.

KUTUZOV. Let them wait. How many men do you think we have lost?

AIDE. Numbers are still coming in. But I think we've lost at least half our effectives. There's scarcely any ammunition left. We need to appoint new officers. So many have been killed. But I think the men would be ready to attack, sir. They sense victory.

KUTUZOV. Half our effectives. Half. If we attack tomorrow, we may lose the other half. Fifty thousand Russians. But if we retreat . . . we sacrifice Moscow. How did this happen? When did it happen? I did not expect this. Not this.

NAPOLEON'S AIDE *approaches.* NAPOLEON *looks gloomy.*

AIDE. Sire . . . Sire.

NAPOLEON. They want more?

AIDE. Sire?

NAPOLEON. They want more! Well, give it them! Send in reinforcements. As many as are required.

BEAUSSET. I hope I may congratulate your majesty on a victory?

NAPOLEON. Go away, you know nothing. (DE BEAUSSET *slopes off.*) Bring me my horse. I'm leaving for Semeonovsk.

PIERRE *suddenly rushes up to him.*

PIERRE. Where are you going? Have you seen what you have done? Go and look at what you've done.

NAPOLEON. Do not imagine that I don't have the stomach for it. I make a point of touring the field of battle once the fighting has stopped. It tests my mind to contemplate the killed and wounded.

PIERRE. Then go! There are a whole army of dead waiting for inspection.

NAPOLEON. I am beginning to think you are wilfully naive. What did you imagine happened in battle? Do you think I take pleasure in this? Well? Twenty of my generals and officers, men I knew personally, friends, are reported dead. We have not captured a single standard. Reinforcements? Never before have I been forced to use so many reinforcements. This is a nightmare.

PIERRE. One of your making. And you accuse me of becoming what I once despised.

NAPOLEON. Do you think I don't dream of returning to my wife and son, of strolling through my gardens in Paris? I am tired.

PIERRE. You are a tyrant!

NAPOLEON. I took on the mantle of power. There must be a visible order. I never claimed otherwise. If I am so wrong, why does half the world applaud me? This is a war for peace. It will establish Europe as a single nation with Paris as the capital and France as the Fatherland. All rivers and seas will be free, all armies reduced, all future wars purely defensive. I am fighting this war for the stability of the world.

PIERRE. No. You are fighting it so that your power will never again be threatened or your will defied.

NAPOLEON. You were not always so blind to my motives. What was it you said? 'For the general good he could not stop short at the life of one man'.

PIERRE (*pointing to the battlefield*). But not this!

NAPOLEON. Who decides where the line should be drawn?

AIDE (*approaching*). Your Majesty, I am honoured to report that the whole of the Russian army has begun to retreat.

Pause.

NAPOLEON. Excellent. In three days I shall be in Moscow.

PIERRE. You realise I am going to have to kill you?

Act Seven

Scene 1

The BEZUHOV *house. St. Petersburg.*

HÉLÈNE *is with her father.*

VASILI. I am only amazed that the fate of Russia could have been entrusted to Kutuzov. A man who cannot sit a horse, who drops asleep at council. A man who cannot see! A fine idea to have a blind general! For what? Blind-man's buff?

HÉLÈNE. Father, you have not listened to a word I have said. I am unwell.

VASILI. I always said Alexander was making a grave mistake. Bagration would have been a better man for the job but now we shall never know. A tragic loss.

HÉLÈNE. Oh, c'est impossible! Mon Dieu, mon Dieu!

VASILI. You know, my dear, at Anna Pavlovna's we pay a forfeit if we catch ourselves speaking French.

HÉLÈNE. I don't care! I don't care about any of it! I don't care if Napoleon takes over the whole world. I am unwell. I have the kind of illness which lasts for nine months, Papa. Nine months. Do you understand?

VASILI (*standing to leave*). I hope you feel better soon, my dear.

HÉLÈNE (*in quiet desperation*). I need a doctor who will be discreet. Someone from abroad. Someone unknown.

VASILI. We have a doctor.

HÉLÈNE. I cannot go through with it, Papa . . .

VASILI. I had better get back to the Palace. There is great alarm, as you can imagine. Terrible times . . .

He leaves.

Scene 2

The ROSTOV *house, Moscow. Everything is in disarray as the family pack up to leave.* SERVANTS *hurry here and there.* SONYA *directs operations.* NATASHA *is sitting amidst her possessions, toying with them and getting nothing done.*

NATASHA. Sonya, you will pack my things for me, won't you?

SONYA. I'm packing all the household items. Couldn't you just make a start? (*She goes on with her work.*)

NATASHA *sighs and flings a few dresses around, hopelessly. She finds the white dress she wore for the ball. She goes to the mirror and holds it up against herself.*

(*Singing feebly.*) Isn't that Natasha Rostova? Yes ... And isn't she a stupid little fool.

She turns away as the COUNTESS, *the* COUNT *and* PETYA *enter.*

COUNTESS. Of all the stupid things you have done, this is the most unforgivable!

COUNT. But I thought you would be pleased. Bezuhov's regiment are in training, they won't see action for months ...

COUNTESS. Pleased? Pleased? You are sending him for a soldier and the milk is hardly dry on his lips?

COUNT. But I'm trying to tell you – he won't see action.

PETYA. I'm going, no matter what, Mama. You can't stop me. I must serve the Fatherland.

COUNTESS. Be quiet, Petya.

PETYA. No, I won't. Fedya Obolensky is going and he's a month younger than me.

COUNTESS. This is all your fault.

COUNT. Mine?

COUNTESS. Yes. With your patriotic talk. 'We must sacrifice everything', you say. Well, we are sacrificing our home, half our belongings, we have given them one son and now you want us to give them the other. I can't sleep even now for worrying about Nikolai. How do you expect me to ... Oh, this is too awful. I'm not leaving here without him.

She runs off. The COUNT *pursues her.*

COUNT. Little Countess, please.

PETYA (*going to* NATASHA). She can't stop me. I've already enrolled. And I'm not going to a regiment in training. I'll transfer. (*About the white dress.*) That's pretty. (*She throws it aside.*) Don't you want it?

NATASHA. No. Why, do you? I'll never wear a dress like that again. It's quite all right. You needn't look so tragic. That part of my life is over.

PETYA. So you're never going to another ball?

NATASHA. No.

PETYA. Or singing another song? Or flirting?

NATASHA. No. Certainly not that.

PETYA. You know, Natalie, I'm terribly proud of you. All my friends think you're lovely. They only come to the house to see you.

NATASHA. Nonsense. They probably think I'm easy prey.

PETYA. No they don't. Some of them know what happened . . .

NATASHA. Don't.

PETYA. But they think it makes you special. Mysterious.

NATASHA. Mysterious?

PETYA. Yes. And one of them said it's no wonder everyone falls in love with you because you're the most beautiful girl he's ever seen.

NATASHA. Who said that?

PETYA. It doesn't matter, does it?

NATASHA. Who said it, Petya?

PETYA. Why?

NATASHA. Just tell me.

PETYA. Why? What do you care? That part of your life is over.

NATASHA (*laughing*). Petya!

PETYA. Ah! I've got you there, haven't I?

NATASHA (*hitting him playfully*). Petya!

PETYA. Ooh . . . I've got you there, cossack!

COUNT (*entering hurriedly*). There's a convoy of wounded in the courtyard. Don't be alarmed. I've told them they can move in here.

PETYA (*running to the window*). Let's see.

COUNT. The streets are full of them and there's nowhere for them to go. Imagine. The French will be here any minute.

NATASHA. That's terrible.

PETYA. Good old Papa.

COUNT. Hurry now everyone. We have to get off.

The COUNT *dashes off again.*

SONYA. Let's go and help them inside. (*She follows.*)

PETYA. Come on.

NATASHA. Petya? You will be careful, won't you? When you go to the regiment, I mean.

PETYA. I don't need to be careful. I'm the Great Petya Rostov! Brother of the beautiful Natasha! I'm invincible!

Scene 3

Outside the house. Bald Hills.

MARIA (*in her white dress*) *accompanied by* MLLE B. *is addressing the peasants. She is nervous.*

MARIA. Please listen to me. The enemy are very close at hand now and it is imperative . . . it is essential that we all leave immediately. Now, I have been told that there are no horses to draw my carriages.

PEASANT. There aren't any.

MARIA. I'm sure some can be found. I thought I saw some this morning, in the far field . . .

PEASANT. There aren't any. They've been taken by the army.

PEASANT. They've been hired out.

MARIA. Please. I'm not intending to leave without you. I ask you to move with all your belongings to our estates beyond Moscow, and there you shall be given housing and food.

PEASANT. We're not going.

MARIA. I can understand that you don't want to leave your homes, but you will fall into enemy hands . . .

PEASANT. The French aren't so bad.

PEASANT (*waving a note*). They gave me a hundred roubles.

PEASANT. If we leave, the Cossacks'll be through to fire the place.

MARIA. What are you talking about?

PEASANT. The Frenchies are at Vislouhovo and they haven't done any harm.

MARIA. Wait. What is this about? Where is your elder?

There are mutterings. The ELDER *is pushed to the front.*

ELDER. We've had a proclamation from the French general. They won't do us any harm. And they'll pay for food or hay they use.

MARIA. But this is impossible! Surely you don't believe them?

MLLE BOURIENNE. Perhaps they are right, chère Princesse. It would be dangerous to go now. There are soldiers and rioters on the road. Perhaps we should appeal to this General. Look, I have a proclamation too. I'm sure all due respect would . . .

MARIA. Where did you get this?

MLLE BOURIENNE. Two men. They must have realised I'm French.

Pause. MARIA struggles to control her fear and anger.

MARIA. I'm not asking this on my own account. I ask in the name of my dead father, who was a good master to you. I have no-one to turn to.

ELDER. We're not following you into penury. I don't care whose name it's in.

MARIA. Then at least let me have some horses so that I may leave.

Pause.

PEASANT. There aren't any horses.

MARIA walks away. MLLE BOURIENNE follows.

MARIA (*suddenly, to* MLLE B). Is there no end to your treachery? You wish me, the daughter of Prince Nikolai Bolkonsky to throw myself for protection on the enemy? You wish them to walk into this house? To sit in my brother's study and amuse themselves by reading his papers? To violate my Father's grave and steal his medals?

MLLE BOURIENNE. Please Princesse, no.

MARIA. I would rather die than bring that shame upon my family.

MLLE BOURIENNE. Please, Princesse, what could I do? I am just a humble woman. I am French. And I miss your father. Let me share your grief. I beg you. I am so afraid.

MARIA embraces her quickly and walks off.

Scene 4

The courtyard. The ROSTOV house. Moscow.

The COUNT is helping to supervise the carts. The COUNTESS enters.

COUNTESS. Servants! Apparently three more of them disappeared during the night. I suppose we must be grateful that they didn't steal anything.

She sees SERVANTS taking trunks back to the house.

Now what's going on? I thought all these had been loaded?
Where's Sonya?

COUNT. Ah . . . yes . . . I was just coming to tell you, little
Countess. We're clearing a few carts for the wounded. We
thought we should take some of them with us. After all, things
are only things and just think what it would . . .

COUNTESS (*to* SERVANTS). Stop! Take them back. All of them.
Now listen to me, Count. There is a hundred thousand roubles'
worth of valuables on those carts. It is the government's job to
look after the wounded so let them get on with it. Take that
back, I say.

NATASHA *enters like a hurricane.*

NATASHA. What's going on? This is awful. It can't be true that
it's by your orders. It isn't, is it, Mama?

COUNTESS. What's the matter with you?

NATASHA. Just come and look at all the wounded in the streets.
They're being left for the French. You can't do it, Mama. What
do we want with all those things, anyway?

COUNTESS. 'Those things', are a life's work. Those things are
your inheritance.

NATASHA. But we don't need them. Oh, please come and look at
the wounded. They're desperate. Mama, we can't.

The COUNTESS *looks to the* COUNT *for support but he averts
his eyes.*

COUNTESS. Oh, do as you please. What do I know? I was wrong
about Petya, now I'm wrong about this.

NATASHA. Mama darling, forgive me.

She goes to embrace her, but the COUNTESS *goes to the*
COUNT.

COUNTESS. Mon cher, you arrange what is right. I don't
understand anything anymore.

COUNT. 'Out of the mouths of babes . . . '

NATASHA *and* PETYA *go back to the carts.*

NATASHA (*to* SERVANTS). Take them back to the house.

SONYA. Excuse me, Mama, Papa, but I thought you should know:
one of the wounded – it's Prince Andrei. He's dying.

COUNTESS (*in dismay*). Natasha?

SONYA. She doesn't know.

COUNTESS. She mustn't be told. Whatever happens, she mustn't
be told.

Scene 5

The courtyard. Bald Hills.

NIKOLAI *and the* ATTENDANT *arrive. The* PEASANTS *eye them suspiciously.*

PEASANT. Which side are you from?

NIKOLAI. The French. And this is Napoleon. What estate is this?

PEASANT. Bald Hills.

NIKOLAI. Why are you people still here? The French are only an hour away. Hurry and get out. Is there any hay?

PEASANT. Maybe there is, maybe there isn't.

MLLE BOURIENNE *comes running up.*

MLLE BOURIENNE. Dear Sir, dear Captain, I am Amelie Bourienne, companion to the Princesse Bolkonskya. The Princesse wishes you to ride up to the house.

NIKOLAI. Bolkonsky, you say?

MLLE BOURIENNE. Yes, sir. Please hurry. She is most distressed.

NIKOLAI. I'll come at once. (*To* PEASANTS.) I'm requisitioning your hay. Show this man where it is.

He leaves with MLLE B.

In the drawing room, the PRINCESS *is waiting.* NIKOLAI *enters and bows.*

NIKOLAI. Captain Rostov, madam. At your service.

MARIA. Captain Rostov? You are not related . . . ?

NIKOLAI. Natasha Rostova is my sister, madam.

MARIA. How strange. I'm sorry we have to meet under such unfortunate circumstances.

NIKOLAI. I have been told of the difficulties you are experiencing.

MARIA. Yes. I'm sure I would not normally be so incapable . . . I mean, I wish I were able to solve them myself. The last few days have been rather trying for me. My father died, you see and . . . (*She cannot go on.*)

NIKOLAI. I cannot express how glad I am, Princess, that I happened to come riding this way and now have the occasion to put myself entirely at your service. You may start from here immediately and I pledge you my word of honour that no-one shall dare to cause you the slightest unpleasantness. If you will allow, I will act as your escort and accompany you as far as I am able.

MARIA. I am very, very grateful to you. I only hope that the whole thing is a misunderstanding and that no-one is to blame. (*She starts to cry.*) Please excuse me.

NIKOLAI. *bows and leaves. He strides over to the* PEASANTS *who have now formed a nervous group.*

NIKOLAI. Where is your elder? (*Before they have chance to answer.*) Caps off, traitors!

They take their caps off, and some begin to bow.

Where is your elder?

ELDER (*stepping forward*). Why, who wants him?

NIKOLAI *deals him a fierce blow round the head which sends him to the ground.*

NIKOLAI. Now. Let's start again, shall we?

Scene 6

In a carriage leaving Moscow.

NATASHA *is sitting with her mother, gazing out of the window at the extraordinary goings on. She sees* PIERRE. *He is wearing an old coat and looks rough and dirty.*

NATASHA. Oh my goodness, it's Pierre. There – in a funny old coat. Look!

COUNTESS. Of course it isn't.

NATASHA. It is. I'd stake my life on it. (*She calls out.*) Piotr Kirillich, come here!

He looks towards her and seems at first not to recognize her. Then the light dawns on him and he moves nearer.

Isn't this wonderful? What are you doing? Why are you dressed like that?

COUNTESS. What has happened, Count?

NATASHA. Are you going to stay in Moscow?

PIERRE. In Moscow. Yes. Goodbye.

NATASHA. Oh, I wish I were a man. I'd stay with you.

COUNTESS. We heard you were at the battle.

NATASHA. But what's the matter, Pierre? Tell me . . .

PIERRE. Don't ask me. I don't know.

COUNTESS. You're walking straight towards the French. And there's a fire!

PIERRE. Goodbye. Goodbye. Terrible times!

COUNTESS. The French are over there!

He stops walking and the carriage leaves him behind. NATASHA looks back at him for as long as possible. He marches purposely through the streets like a man possessed. People scatter out of his way and look at him strangely. NAPOLEON appears some distance away.

NAPOLEON. Still planning to kill me?

PIERRE (*not looking at him*). I will kill you. I'll kill you with this dagger and as I strike the blow, I'll say, 'Not I, but the hand of Providence punishes thee'.

NAPOLEON. You would do better with a pistol. A student in Vienna tried with a dagger. They shot him.

PIERRE. Let them shoot me.

NAPOLEON. It is not in your nature to kill me. You will not sacrifice life for principal as we have already seen. You would plunge that knife into my flesh? You would watch the blood gush forth? Would you?

PIERRE. Yes. I will deliver all Europe from her misery.

NAPOLEON. Your heart is as soft as your belly. You will not kill in cold blood.

PIERRE. My blood isn't cold; it's boiling.

By now PIERRE has reached the very centre of the area where the fire is raging. The noise is tremendous. Terrified people run to and fro with their belongings. Some are fighting over things, some are standing and weeping. Here and there, French soldiers can be seen, looting.

A WOMAN suddenly flings herself at PIERRE's feet.

WOMAN. Help me, kind sir. My baby, my little one!

PIERRE. What is it? Where is your baby?

WOMAN. Left behind. Burning to death. Merciful Heavens, help me!

PIERRE. Which house? Which house? Show me and I'll go.

WOMAN (*pointing*). There!

PIERRE runs towards the house.

Oh good, kind sir! Good benefactor! God bless you!

PIERRE. *looks for a way into the burning house. There is a crash – a whole drawer full of silver lands at his feet.*

French SOLDIERS *above him are shouting and laughing.* PIERRE *finds a way through to the back of the house. He jumps over a fence. The child is sitting on the ground, screaming. He snatches it up. It struggles and tries to bite him but he holds on. He makes it back to where the woman accosted him. She has gone. He looks about in dismay.*

Not far away two French SOLDIERS *are harrassing an OLD MAN and his DAUGHTER. One* SOLDIER *takes the OLD MAN's boots, the other circles the girl ominously. He suddenly grabs her and wrenches a necklace from her throat. She screams.* PIERRE *throws the child into the arms of a bystander and runs at the* SOLDIER.

PIERRE. Leave that woman alone!

He knocks the SOLDIER *to the ground and a fight ensues.* PIERRE *fights with super-human strength.*

A well-ordered patrol of French SOLDIERS *appears on the scene.* PIERRE *is restrained. His arms are bound. He is searched. They find the dagger.*

OFFICER. Do you speak French? What is your name?

PIERRE. I will not tell you my name. I am your prisoner.

OFFICER. Your name?

PIERRE. I will not tell you my name.

OFFICER. Another incendiary. Take him!

He is led off.

Scene 7

Inside a hut. Great Mytischy. Fourteen miles from Moscow.

It is night. The COUNTESS *is lying on a mattress trying to sleep.* NATASHA *sits on some straw, plaiting her hair with a fixed intensity.* SONYA, *in her nightdress, is looking out of the window. From a hut nearby comes the sound of a man groaning piteously and incessantly.*

SONYA. It's awful. The whole of Moscow is in flames. Imagine if we were still there . . . Natasha, do come and look. Natasha?

NATASHA *glances up then goes on with her plait.*

NATASHA. Oh yes.

SONYA. But you didn't see.

COUNTESS. She doesn't want to look. For goodness sake, come to bed now and let us all get some sleep.

SONYA *gets into bed.* NATASHA *goes to the window and looks out. She begins to sob, quietly.*

COUNTESS. Natasha. Natasha, please don't cry.

NATASHA. Is that him? Just tell me. It's him, isn't it?

COUNTESS. Oh my pet, is that what's been worrying you? It isn't him. It's another of the wounded. I should have said.

NATASHA. I want to see him.

COUNTESS. No. I've told you, it's out of the question. There's nothing you can do. If I ever find out who told you . . .

NATASHA. It doesn't matter.

COUNTESS. I have my suspicions, of course.

NATASHA. I'm glad I know. I'm not a child anymore.

COUNTESS. I know you're not. Why don't you come and share the bed? We'll cuddle up like we used to?

NATASHA. I'm fine here. Thank you.

COUNTESS. Well, then. Let's all get some sleep. We've got another long journey tomorrow.

All three of them settle down. NATASHA *lies still. She waits until her mother's breathing sounds regular. She sits up.*

SONYA (*whispering*). Are you all right?

She doesn't reply. She gets up silently and steals from the room. SONYA *watches her leave.*

A light appears over where PRINCE ANDREI *is lying.* NATASHA *feels her way towards it. She is frightened of the dark and of what she will find when she reaches him but she has to go on. She sees him. He is sitting up slightly in bed and he watches her approach. He isn't sure if she is real at first, but as she gets nearer he sighs with relief and happinesss as if he was waiting for her. He smiles and holds out his hand. She falls to her knees beside him.*

ANDREI. You. What happiness!

NATASHA. Forgive me. Forgive me.

ANDREI. Forgive what?

NATASHA. Forgive me for what I did.

ANDREI. I love you more. Better than before. Love is everything, Natasha. Love is what binds us to life. Love is God. I know that now.

NATASHA *sobs and kisses his hand. Throughout the next scenes we see her nursing him.*

Scene 8

A drum begins to beat. PIERRE is taken to the Dyevichy Meadow where he joins five other PRISONERS. There is a post in the ground and beyond it a pit has been dug. A crowd looks on. To the right and left of the post, stands a company of French SOLDIERS with muskets.

The AIDE places the prisoners in numerical order according to a list. PIERRE is placed sixth.

AIDE (*to* PIERRE). What is your name?

The first two PRISONERS are taken and tied to the post. One keeps crossing himself, the other scratches his shoulder and tries to smile. Sacks are put over their heads and tied.

Six SOLDIERS step forward and halt, eight paces form the post. PIERRE looks down. They fire. The bodies slump. SOLDIERS untie them with trembling hands and throw them into the pit.

The next two PRISONERS are led to the post and the whole thing is repeated.

AIDE (*to* PIERRE). What is your name?

PIERRE (*afraid*). My name is Bezuhov. I am Count Bezuhov. Count Bezuhov.

AIDE (*to* SOLDIER). Just the boy.

The fifth PRISONER is a young factory-hand. As the SOLDIERS try to lead the boy forward, he clings to PIERRE in terror. PIERRE shudders and shakes him off.

He is dragged to the post and tied. He suddenly becomes meek and stands quietly as the sack is placed over his head. He rubs one bare foot against the other.

This time, PIERRE watches as the soldiers fire – though he hears nothing. He simply sees the body sag against the ropes and blood appear.

PIERRE rushes to the post. No-one stops him. The hands of the soldiers shake as they untie the boy and throw him into the pit. PIERRE looks down. The boy is still twitching convulsively as earth begins to rain down.

PIERRE is taken back to his place. The troops withdraw, running in pairs. One young soldier however, stays still, staring at the post. Another has to seize him and pull him into line.

The crowd disperses.

AIDE. That'll teach them to start fires.

PIERRE *looks at him and sees in his eyes that he is ashamed and is trying to justify the executions to himself.*

PIERRE *has become numb. He is in profound shock. He is taken to a prison-hut and thrown in. He falls to the ground and curls up like a baby.*

Scene 9

The prison-hut. Moscow.

PIERRE *is still lying on the ground in the same position. He opens his eyes then closes them. After a moment, he opens them again. It is almost dark in the hut. He becomes aware of voices around him – those of his fellow* PRISONERS. *There is intermittent laughter and here and there a candle flickers.*

Nearby, sits a small man. He is doing something to his legs and PIERRE *gradually discerns that he is taking off his leg-bands. He does so in a careful, systematic way, which fascinates* PIERRE. *It is calm and ordered – deft circular movements of the arm. He hangs up each leg-band in turn on two pegs above his sack. He sits still and looks at* PIERRE.

KARATAEV. You've seen a lot of trouble, sir, eh?

PIERRE *is taken unawares by the kindness of this sing-song voice. Tears well in his eyes.*

Eh lad, don't fret now. Suffering lasts an hour but life goes on forever. That's the way it is. And we live here without offence. There are good men amongst us as well as bad.

He crosses the hut and returns with a piece of rag in his hand, which he unwraps to reveal pieces of cooked potato. He passes the rag carefully to PIERRE.

Here, you have a taste of this, sir. We had soup for dinner and the potatoes are grand.

The potatoes smell wonderful to PIERRE. *He takes one and begins to eat.*

All right, then, are they? You're eating them wrong, you know. You should do it like this.

He takes out his clasp-kife, and cuts a potato in half. He takes salt from the rag, sprinkles it on and hands it back.

They're grand. Eat them like that. (PIERRE *does so. They are grand.*) And how came they to arrest you, my friend? (PIERRE *is silent. He has forgotten how to speak.*) We're all soldiers. From the Aspheron Regiment. There were twenty or more of us lying sick in the hospital when they fetched us here. My name's

Platon. Platon Karataev. So, you must have a family estate, sir.
And a house. And a wife, maybe? And your old parents still alive?

Pause.

PIERRE. My parents are dead.

KARATAEV. I'm sorry, sir. No mother, then? I'm sorry. A wife
for good sense, a mother-in-law for a kind welcome, but there's
none so dear as a man's own mother. And have you little'uns?
(PIERRE *shakes his head.*) Never mind. You're still young.

PIERRE. It makes no difference now.

KARATAEV. Ah, my friend. You can never be sure a beggar's
sack or a prison-house won't fall to your lot. The great thing is
to live in harmony. (*He settles himself more comfortably.*) Take
me, for instance. I went with my young brother into a neighbour's
copse after wood. We were caught by the bee-keeper. Well, we
were flogged and tried and I, being oldest, was shaved and sent
for a soldier. Now that may seem hard, but it turned out to be a
blessing. If it hadn't been me, it would have been my brother
who had to go and he has five little 'uns. I just left a wife
behind – we had a little girl once but the Lord took her. Now
I comes home on my first leave and what do you think? I finds
them all better off then they was before. Yard full of livestock,
women-folk at home, and the little 'uns all helping on the farm.
And that's the way it is, my good sir. There's no escaping fate.
But we're always finding fault and complaining: this ain't right
and the other don't suit. Happiness, friend, is like water in a net
– pull it along behind you and it bulges: take it out and it's
empty. Well, I daresay you're sleepy. (*He crosses himself.*)
Lord Jesus Christ, holy St.Nikola, Frola and Lavra. Lord Jesus
Christ, holy St.Nikola, Frola and Lavra. Lord Jesus Christ have
mercy on us and save us! (*He touches the ground with his
forehead and settles on his sack.*) Lay me down like a stone,
O God, and raise me up like new bread.

He pulls his coat over himself and falls asleep. PIERRE *sits
still. Noises of crying and screaming drift in. The* FACTORY-
LAD *appears in the darkness. He is covered in dirt and blood.
He begins to choke. He opens his mouth and spits dirt. He holds
out a hand to* PIERRE. PIERRE *suddenly begins to cry loudly.*

KARATAEV (*waking*). Don't fret, sir.

PIERRE. They shouldn't have done it. They shouldn't have shot
those men. The last was just a lad, just a boy. And I kept
asking, who is doing this? Who is it that wants this? And no-
one did. Not the ones who pulled the triggers, not the Marshal
who sentenced us, not Napoleon, not anyone. But we did it. We
all stood round and did it. And their lives were gone. What are
we? What are we?

KARATAEV. Now, now, my friend . . .

PIERRE. You don't understand. He clung to me, but I shook him off. And he wasn't even dead. And they shovelled dirt on his face.

KARATAEV. Now, now. You're sad. How can we not be sad in times like these? But the boy will be with God.

PIERRE. There is no God.

KARATAEV. Don't say so, good sir. There is only God and he is merciful. We cannot shape the way things are. It's all as He disposes. The great thing is to live in harmony. To live in harmony and to give Him thanks. Tomorrow you will wake and be thirsty and you'll be given tea. And when you're so hungry that you think you'll cave-in, you'll be given food. And there's a little dog – perhaps she'll come to visit us and she makes us all smile. And they'll let us out for air, and you can see the hoar-frost on the Sparrow Hills and hear the jackdaws cawing in the trees above the river. Don't fret, sir. Go to sleep now. Lay me down like a stone, O God, and raise me up like new bread.

He lies down. Pause.

PIERRE. Lay me down like a stone, O God, and raise me up like new bread. (*He lies down. The noises drift in.*) Terrible sounds.

KARATAEV. Don't listen. Don't listen.

PIERRE *puts his hands over his ears, and sleeps.*

During the next few scenes, we see him learning from KARATAEV and adjusting to his new life.

Scene 10

A church. Voronezh. MARIA is praying. Little NIKOLAI sits behind her, also trying to pray.

NIKOLAI *enters and pauses for a moment, watching MARIA. Little NIKOLAI turns and sees him. He nudges his aunt.*

MARIA. Captain Rostov.

NIKOLAI. Have no fear, Princess, I have not been following you across Russia. (*They both blush awkwardly.*) I'm sorry to interrupt . . .

MARIA. No . . .

NIKOLAI. I have some news of your brother.

MARIA. He's not . . . ? Oh, please God . . .

NIKOLAI. No. No, not that. He is with my parents. I had a letter from them. They are at Yaroslavl.

MARIA. With your parents? You know he was wounded? I read it in the newspaper.

NIKOLAI. Yes. Natasha is nursing him. My mother says his condition is serious but that it has improved somewhat of late. It seems he travelled with them from Moscow.

MARIA. I must start for Yaroslavl.

NIKOLAI. Is this his son?

MARIA *nods. He stoops and ruffles the boy's hair.*

He is like him.

MARIA. It seems I am indebted to you again.

NIKOLAI. Not at all. I thought you should know immediately. Of course, I could have written but . . . well, with news of this import . . .

MARIA (*almost smiling*). I quite understand. Thank you.

NIKOLAI. Well, I shall leave you in peace. (*He kisses her hand and leaves.*)

MARIA. Peace? (*To God.*) Did you send him to me? I love him. And if he doesn't love me and nothing ever happens, what harm will it do? I will love him until the day I die.

Scene 11

A house. Yaroslavl. MARIA *has just arrived. The* COUNTESS *is with her.* NATASHA *runs in.* MARIA *looks into her eyes and then rushes to her. They embrace. Little* NIKOLAI *looks on. The* COUNTESS *leaves them alone.*

MARIA. How is he?

NATASHA (*shakes her head*). I can't say exactly. He seemed happy before . . . we even talked of the future . . . but then, two days ago, this suddenly happened.

MARIA. What? Has he grown weaker?

NATASHA. No. It's not that. (*She leads her towards where* ANDREI *is lying.*) Oh, Maria, he has left us. He has left us already.

MARIA *approaches* ANDREI. *He looks at her slowly and with what seems like hostility. She grows nervous.*

ANDREI. How are you, Marie? How did you get here?

MARIA. How are you now?

ANDREI. That, my dear, you must ask the doctor.

Pause.

NATASHA. Marie came by Ryazan.

ANDREI. Really? So, you have met Count Nikolai. He wrote that he took a great liking to you. It would be a good thing if you were to marry.

MARIA (*glancing at* NATASHA). Why talk of me? (*Pause.*) Andrei, would you like to see little Nikolai? He's here. He's always asking about you.

ANDREI (*smiling ironically*). Yes. I should like to see little Nikolai.

MARIA *leads the boy forward.* ANDREI *kisses him, but neither of them speak.* MARIA *begins to cry.*

ANDREI. He won't have a father. Is that why you're crying? (MARIA *nods.*) Marie, you know that in the Bible it says . . .

He does not go on.

MARIA. Yes?

ANDREI. Nothing. You mustn't cry. You mustn't cry here.

Scene 12

The throne room. The Kremlin. NAPOLEON *paces the room, his calf twitching.* DE BEAUSSET *sits languidly in a corner. The* AIDE-DE-CAMP *is reading reports from various sections of the army authorities.*

AIDE. 'Looting continues in the city. Order is not yet restored and there is not a single merchant engaging in legitimate trade.'

Shall I go on, Sire? (*No reply.*)

'The Grand Marshal of the Palace complains bitterly that, despite repeated prohibitions, the soldiers continue to perform the offices of nature in all the courtyards, and even under the Emperor's very windows.' (DE BEAUSSET *tuts.*) 'In the Old Guard, the disorder and pillage have been more violent than ever last night and . . .'

NAPOLEON. Tell the Old Guard immediately that I look to them as the élite who guard my person, my person, to set an example and that from now on, any insubordination will be punishable by death. Do you understand?

AIDE. Yes, Sire.

NAPOLEON. This must stop. This must stop. This must stop. Normal life must be resumed. I want this city back. Why has trade not been re-established? What has happened to the proclamation I sent out to the artisans and peasants?

AIDE. There has been no response, Sire. And many of the commissioners who took it into the countryside were killed.

BEAUSSET. Perhaps they have realised that our roubles are counterfeit.

NAPOLEON. Why are the churches not resuming services?

AIDE. One or two are, Sire.

NAPOLEON. Where are the theatres and the clubs?

AIDE. We have re-opened a theatre in the Kremlin.

BEAUSSET. I went last night but the show was cancelled. Apparently the actors had been robbed of their posessions.

NAPOLEON. I did not build an Empire on anarchy, I built it on discipline and order! (*He paces the room.*) What is Kutuzov doing? What is his plan? Why does he not take action?

BEAUSSET. Does anyone actually know where the Russian army is?

NAPOLEON. You should rather be asking where the French army is! I see only criminals and marauders!

Well if he refuses to make a move, I shall have to.

Scene 13

The prison-hut. Moscow.

There is the sound of commotion from outside.

The PRISONERS *are packing up their precious belongings and pulling on extra clothing.*

PIERRE *enters. He has a beard and his hair is unkempt. His overcoat is tied with a length of rope.*

KARATAEV. What's happening?

PIERRE. They're pulling out. The whole army. They're taking us with them.

PRISONER. It can't be true.

PIERRE. The French are retreating.

There is a cheer from the prisoners.

PRISONER Why would they retreat now? I thought they'd press on to Petersburg.

KARATAEV. The maggot that gnaws the cabbage always dies first.

PIERRE. They've got orders to shoot anyone who falls behind. We've got to hurry.

The PRISONERS *resume their preparations.*

KARATAEV (*handing* PIERRE *shoes made from scraps of leather*). Here, my friend. Tie them tight.

PIERRE. How are you?

KARATAEV. How am I? Grumble at sickness and God won't grant you death.

The sound of a beating drum is heard. It continues through the next few scenes.

Scene 14

With the Russian army, near Moscow. KUTUZOV *falls to his knees before the icon.*

KUTUZOV. Oh Lord, my Creator, Thou hast heard our prayer. Russia is saved! I thank Thee, O Lord! (*He weeps.*)

Scene 15

On the Kaluga highway.

It is snowing. PIERRE *and the* PRISONERS *are marching. The drum is beating. The French* SOLDIERS *keep them moving along.* KARATAEV *stops and sits on the ground. He is ill and cannot go on.* PIERRE *turns and looks at him.* KARATAEV's *eyes seem to be beckoning him but* PIERRE *covers his ears and keeps walking. The corporal and another soldier go back to* KARATAEV *and try, unsuccessfully, to get him up. The* CORPORAL *shoots him.*

The SOLDIERS *rejoin the convoy.* PIERRE *looks at the* CORPORAL *but the* CORPORAL *looks away.*

Scene 16

Yaroslavl.

PRINCE ANDREI *dies.* MARIA, NATASHA, *little* NIKOLAI, SONYA, *the* COUNT *and* COUNTESS, *stand around the bed in silence.*

NATASHA *closes his eyes and hugs his body. Little* NIKOLAI *begins to cry and* MARIA *takes his hand.*

Scene 17

The Kaluga highway. Night. PIERRE is sitting next to a camp fire, a short distance away from some other prisoners.

NAPOLEON appears. PIERRE looks at him uninterestedly and then back at the fire. He begins to laugh. Quietly at first, then louder.

NAPOLEON. What's so funny?

PIERRE. You took me and shut me up. You kept me prisoner. What, me? Me? My immortal soul? Perhaps I will never be completely happy or completely free, but I need never be unhappy either, and nobody can own me!

He laughs so loudly that others look at him in amazement. He looks up at the sky.

All that is mine. All that is in me, and all that is me. And you took all that and shut it in a shed and barricaded it with planks so it couldn't get out! (*He laughs and laughs.*)

PIERRE *and the* PRISONERS *settle down to sleep. In the darkness* DOLOHOV, PETYA *and other* PARTISANS *creep forward.* DOLOHOV *struggles to restrain* PETYA.

DOLOHOV. Wait, Petya. Wait, Petya.

Suddenly PETYA *cries out.*

PETYA. Hurra-a-h!

He brandishes his sword exactly as he did when, as a boy, he imagined himself as NIKOLAI *in action.*

He charges down the hill. The others follow. The French hastily grab their swords and muskets.

Everything goes into slow motion. PETYA *is shot. He falls.*

The French are quickly overpowered. The PRISONERS *emerge from where they have taken cover.*

DOLOHOV *goes over to where* PETYA *is lying.*

DOLOHOV. Done for.

PIERRE, *seeing* DOLOHOV, *approaches. Then he sees* PETYA.

PIERRE. Petya Rostov.

Scene 18

Yaroslavl.

The whole house is filled by a terrible, piercing scream.

NATASHA *comes running and meets her father, who is leaving her mother's room. His face is contorted with grief. On seeing* NATASHA, *he waves his arms despairingly and breaks into convulsive, painful sobs.*

COUNT. Pe . . . Petya. Go to her . . . go . . . she is callling you. (*Weeping like a child, he totters to a chair and covers his face with his hands.*)

NATASHA *steps nearer to her mother's room. Princess* MARIA *comes out, her face full of tears. She takes her hands and speaks but* NATASHA *cannot really hear.*

MARIA. If there is anything I can do . . . anything, my love.

NATASHA *enters her mother's room. Her mother is sitting in a chair. Her body is stiff and awkward and she beats her head against the chair back.* SONYA, *is holding her arms, trying to calm her.*

COUNTESS. Natasha! Natasha! It's not true. They're lying to me. Go away, get away from me.

She pushes SONYA *from her.* SONYA *leaves and goes to the* COUNT. NATASHA *kneels down by her mother and takes her in her arms.*

NATASHA. Mamma, my darling . . . I'm here, I'm here.

COUNTESS (*suddenly taking hold of* NATASHA's *face and staring into her eyes*). Natasha, you love me, you would not deceive me. You will tell me the truth.

NATASHA (*beginning to cry*). Mamma . . . dearest . . .

COUNTESS (*letting go.*) Oh no . . . oh no . . . my boy . . . my baby . . .

COUNT. All my life I have tried to protect her. All my life. I have not been strong . . . not noble . . . all I wanted was for her to be happy. Oh, Petya. Petya.

Scene 19

Yaroslavl.

NATASHA *is still sitting in the same position, holding her mother, who has fallen asleep.* SONYA *creeps into the room.*

SONYA. You must rest now. I'll sit with her.

NATASHA. Stay with me. I'm not sleepy.

SONYA. Please go and lie down. You're shivering. I'll come for you if she wakes, I promise. (NATASHA *takes her arms from*

around her mother.) Natasha, I just wanted to tell you . . . I
have written to Nikolai releasing him from our engagement. I
know it's what Mama wants and . . . she has so little now.

NATASHA *kisses her and leaves.*

Scene 20

ANNA PAVLOVNA SCHERER's *drawing room. St. Petersburg.*

ANNA PAVLOVNA *and* PRINCE VASILI *sit together drinking
tea.*

VASILI. The order of St. George. First class.

ANNA. He deserves no less. Mihail Kutuzov shall go down as one
of the *plus grands hommes d'histoire.*

VASILI. They do say that he sobbed when the Emperor embraced
him. I always had faith in him.

ANNA. He has not only saved Russia, he has saved all Europe.

VASILI. I suppose the army will pursue Bonaparte to Paris.

ANNA. Yes. How quiet it will be. (*Pause.*)

VASILI. I never expected this, you know, ma chère: to be alone in
my old-age. I never expected to outlive my children.

ANNA. My poor Vasili. Anatole died a valiant death.

VASILI. Yes. But I can't help feeling just a little guilty about
Hélène.

ANNA. But what could you have done? Angina pectoris is a
terrible affliction.

VASILI. Still, she was very beautiful, wasn't she?

ANNA. Very.

Scene 21

The BOLKONSKY *house. Moscow.*

PIERRE *is waiting. He is in black. Although his beard has gone
and his hair is tidy, he still bears some of the signs of his
adventure. He is thinner, and more animated.*

The ATTENDANT *approaches.*

PIERRE. Will she see me?

ATTENDANT. Yes, Your Excellency. Please step into the portrait
gallery.

PIERRE *does so. There, in a dim light, he sees* MARIA, *sitting with, whom he assumes to be, her companion. They are both in black.* MARIA *rises and approaches.*

MARIA. So this is how we meet again. Andrei often talked of you, even towards the end. (*She glances at her companion.*) I was so glad to hear of your safety. It was the only piece of good news we had for a long time.

PIERRE. I knew nothing. I thought he had been killed. Then I heard that he had fallen in with the Rostovs. What a strange coincidence.

MARIA *looks embarrassed. She gazes round at her companion.*

MARIA. You don't recognize her, do you?

PIERRE *looks at the woman. She is pale and thin and yet there is something familiar about her. Suddenly he realises.*

PIERRE. Natasha!

She steps forward, shyly. He goes to her and takes both her hands in his and does not let go.

Epilogue

Bald Hills. December 1820.

Eight years have passed. In the drawing room, the family are gathered around the samovar.

NATASHA. – *pregnant – is looking joyfully at* PIERRE. *He has just returned from St. Petersburg.*

NIKOLAI's *solid presence leaves no doubt that this is his estate, his drawing room.*

MARIA *is sitting contentedly with a baby on her lap.*

SONYA *presides over the samovar.*

The COUNTESS ROSTOVA, *who now looks like an old lady, is asleep in a chair.*

PIERRE. The Emperor has let everything go. All he asks for is peace, and he can only get peace through these men of no faith and no conscience – I mean men like Arackcheyev and Magnitsky, who recklessly hack at and strangle everything. If you didn't look after Bald Hills yourself, and only asked for a quiet life, you would employ the most savage bailiff you could find so as to keep things in order. You must see that.

NIKOLAI. I can't believe that things are as bad as you claim.

PIERRE. That's because you never go to St. Petersburg.

NATASHA. Whilst you go far too often.

PIERRE. We live a very sheltered life here, you know? (*To* NATASHA.) Are you ever going to forgive me for staying away?

NATASHA. No. I might. (PIERRE *smiles.*) It's all very well for you, you were having a good time. But what about me? You might at least show some consideration for your children. Petya has been at death's door.

PIERRE. I'm sorry. I'm here now. And just in time for Nikolai's birthday.

NIKOLAI. Well, come on, Pierre, explain to me exactly what is so bad, and how you think you could improve it.

MARIA. Perhaps we should wait until later . . .

PIERRE. I'd rather not go into it now.

NIKOLAI. If you're worried about your secret society, I don't think anyone here is going to run to the authorities.

PIERRE. All right then: there is larceny in the law-courts, in the army nothing but flogging and forced labour in military settlements. And as for the so-called Bible Association! Arakcheyev and Golitsyn practically own the government. They see conspiracy everywhere and in everything. Civilisation is being crushed.

COUNTESS (*awakening*). What fault could anyone find with Prince Golitsyn? He is a most estimable man. I used to meet him in the old days at Maria Antonovna's. (*Awkward silence.*) And a Bible Association – what harm is there in that?

NIKOLAI. You see Maman, the association has great influence, so they say.

COUNTESS. Nowadays people find fault with everyone. I'm going to bed. Birthday tomorrow, Nikolai. (*She stands with* SONYA's *help.*) Are you going to sing, Natasha?

NATASHA. Oh, I doubt it. I'm so out of practice. Perhaps.

COUNTESS. Your father did so love to hear you sing.

She heads for the door. People call 'goodnight'.

SONYA. Shall I take the baby to the nursery, Maria?

MARIA (*handing him over*). Yes. Thank you.

SONYA *and the* COUNTESS *leave.*

NATASHA. What a heart dear Sonya has.

There is general agreement. The ATTENDANT *enters and begins to tidy things up in preparation for closing the gallery.*

PIERRE. In my opinion, the strain is too great and something is going to give way.

NIKOLAI. Is that what your secret society says?

PIERRE. Yes.

NIKOLAI. So what will it do? What are its aims? You see, in my 'sheltered' opinion, a secret society must necessarily be a mischievous one, which can only breed evil.

NATASHA. Nikolai, really! If Pierre is involved with it, it must be good.

PIERRE. On the contrary, we are gentlemen in the true sense of the word. Many of us were officers who fought with you at Borodino. We stand for love and mutual help.

NIKOLAI. And what does that mean, exactly? In practice.

PIERRE. That is what we have been debating. Many of us feel that the time has come for direct action.

NIKOLAI. Meaning what?

PIERRE. Revolution.

Pause. The ATTENDANT *drops something on the floor.*

NIKOLAI. For God's sake, do you have to make so much noise?

ATTENDANT. Sorry, sir.

NIKOLAI. Don't be so damned clumsy.

He glances at MARIA. *She shakes her head, almost imperceptibly, as if to say, 'don't'. The* ATTENDANT *leaves.*

Let me tell you this, Pierre: You are my best friend, as you know, but if your secret society began working against the government – any government – I know it would be my duty to obey that government. And if Arakcheyev bid me lead a squadron against you and mow you down, I shouldn't hesitate for a second, I should do it!

Music. NATASHA *and* PIERRE *sit at one side of the stage,* MARIA *and* NIKOLAI *at the other.*

NIKOLAI. Natasha is too absurd. We know she can twist him round her little finger, but when it comes to ideas she just assumes that everything he says is right!

MARIA. For what it's worth, I completely agreed with you. Pierre is a good man, he believes it is our duty to help our neighbour, but he forgets that we have other duties nearer home which God himself has marked out for us. We may run risks for ourselves but we have our children to think about now.

NIKOLAI. That's exactly what I said! Well, it's exactly what I wish I'd said. You are so wise. It frightens me sometimes.

MARIA. You know, my love . . .

NIKOLAI. I know what you're going to say.

MARIA. Please try not to be so harsh with the servants.

NIKOLAI. I do.

MARIA. If you feel you can't control yourself, you must walk away, walk away as fast as you can.

NATASHA. The problem with Nikolai is that unless a thing is generally accepted, he will never agree to it.

PIERRE. No, the truth of the matter is that to Nikolai, ideas and discussions are only an amusement but to me they are everything. When I was in Petersburg I felt – I can say this to you – I felt that without me the whole thing would fall apart. I succeeded in uniting them all.

NATASHA. I'm sure you did.

NIKOLAI. What do I care what goes on in St. Petersburg or whether Arakcheyev is a villain? You know, all I want is to make this estate work, to repay you and not leave my children such paupers as I was left myself. (MARIA *is beaming at him.*) What? What?

MARIA (*kissing his hand*). Nothing. Even in my dreams, I never knew I could be so happy.

The ATTENDANT *enters and begins to turn out the lights.*

NATASHA. Do you know what I'm thinking about? Platon Karateyev. What would he have said? Would he have approved of you now?

PIERRE. I don't know . . . No, he wouldn't have approved. He would have approved of us, our family life. He was always so keen to find harmony and peace in everything. But he wouldn't approve of the society. But what can I do, Natasha? All ideas which have great results are simple. My idea is just that if vicious people unite together into a power, then honest people must do the same. That's simple enough, isn'it?

The lights go out.

End.